HORROR STORIES

TERRIFYINGLY REAL STORIES OF TRUE HORROR & CHILLING MURDERS

HANNAH J TIDY

CONTENTS

INTRODUCTION

True Story! "A killer stayed in a family's house for hours, eating their food, logging into their computer, and sleeping on their couch. It's so eerie because rarely does a killer stick around for hours after they commit their crime, making themselves at home." Creepy! The world can be a crazy place; stories such as these give people a glimpse into the minds of people who witness or committed these fundamental taboos.

My name is Hannah J Tidy, let me start our night of horror by telling you, this collection of the darkest true crime and paranormal horror stories is not a work of fiction. From mass murders, mysterious deaths, to possessed hotels and creepy online forums, you will be clinging to the edge of your seat, while looking over your shoulder. These are true-to-life, real accounts, verbally passed on from generation to generation, written about in old newspaper accounts all over the world, researched and factually documented, and presented to you, in all their darkest and unblemished retelling and anguished glory. I wish I could say these stories of mass murders, cannibalism, houses with bleeding walls, mysterious deaths, malicious evil apparitions, and the like, we're all just a figment of our imagination. But that is not the case. Many people believe in the existence of ghosts, supernatural beings, and spirits from beyond this world.

These stories solidify that claim, bringing to life the unexplainable. So, while reading, please remember that I did warn you. These stories retold over time, taken from old newspaper clippings and heard about from real witness accounts, will make you want to close your eyes on the horror that is unexplained and the unknown. Who knows what lies in the darkest corners of our everyday lives? Are you feeling goosebumps prickle on your arms and back just yet? You might start to question if the devil is real if demons exist and if they're genuinely is hell.

Come, it's time. I hope you enjoy the book, but don't forget to keep your lights, keeping the shadows at bay. So, sit back relax, It's going to be a long night.

1

FARM STRAIGHT FROM HELL

On a quiet night on March 31, 1922, in a small, unassuming farmstead between the Bavarian towns of Ingolstadt and Schrobenhausen (around 70 km north of Munich), one of the most terrifying and mysteriously unsolved murders in Germany chillingly took place. Was this the work of the devil or someone who seemed to do his evil bidding? On that quiet evening, different darkness descended on the small farmstead called Hinterkaifeck, and tragically, there was no one around that night to hear the horrified screaming and agonized suffering of the victims. Piercing screams unanswered in the cold night air, together with the ominous thud of the *mattock* (or a German pickaxe), the impact fatal on human skin and bone, as the unknown killer brutally and systematically slaughtered all the inhabitants one by one. These were the only terrible sounds that night in the Hinterkaifeck farmstead. After that, a haunting silence for the next few days.

The unfortunate family who lived on Hinterkaifeck Farm were the Grubers; Andreas (63) was a farmer, husband to Cäzilia (72), and father to their widowed daughter Viktoria Gabriel (35) who was the official owner of the Hinterkaifeck farm. Viktoria lived with her mother and father on the farmstead, along with her two young children, Cäzilia (7) and Josef (2). On that terrible and mysterious night, the new maid, Maria Baumgartner (44), who arrived at the household only a few hours before, was also an unfortunate victim in the savage slaying in Hinterkaifeck farmstead.

Andreas Gruber and the entire Gruber family were known to be quite well off in the area, but not particularly well-liked among the townspeople. The family lived a considerable distance outside of town, with the farmstead quietly hidden within the forest, and they were known by the villagers to be reclusive and mostly kept to themselves. The home was far off from their nearest neighbors. But, the lives of the Gruber family were still a much-talked-about topic in town. Andreas regularly beat his wife, Cäzilia, and also had a long history of being brutal and maltreating his children in the past. Viktoria was the only surviving child of her father's cruel punishment and parenting style; none of her other siblings survived the vicious beatings. But, amidst all this old talk and scandal, the moral reason that genuinely shocked the sensibilities of the rural towns-people and affected how they felt towards the Gruber family, was the alleged abusive relationship between Andreas and his only daughter, Viktoria. This practice was illegal but, unfortunately, still fairly commonplace in rural towns like theirs. Lorenz Schlittenbauer, a neighboring farmer, officially admitted that he was the father of young Josef, that was not enough to quell the rumors and hushed talk that Viktoria's young son, was the incestuous fruit of the illicit relationship between Viktoria and her father. Andreas was also said to be obsessed with Viktoria and sternly forbade her even to get remarried after she became a widow. But, like a true lady of good stock, despite all the talk and rumor-mongering in town, Viktoria held herself above the malicious fray and often attended Church services. She even became an active member of the Church choir with her beautiful singing voice. After some time, the community eventually accepted Viktoria. She had her place, despite her family background, because of her steadfast devotion to the Church and constant attendance at service.

But, back at the Hinterkaifeck farm, things started to take a slow, ominous turn for the worse. One day, the Gruber household maid quit her job and requested to leave almost immediately. The maid stated, she no longer wanted to work in the home because of the strange sounds and voices she heard, as well as footsteps echoing from the empty attic. Convinced there was a haunting in the house, she no longer felt safe staying there. Witnesses stated that the maid was pale and emaciated when she left, looking as if she had been through nights of pure horror at the farm.

The Grubers did not take the maid's stories seriously and even believed that she must have been mentally disturbed.

About six months later, another strange and mysterious occurrence materialized in Hinterkaifeck. Andreas Gruber was outside in the farm, making rounds and walking in the front yard near the woods when he discovered odd-shaped footprints in the snow. He followed the strange tracks until he reached the main house and saw that the footprints led directly to his front door. Andreas was quite concerned at that point because he looked all over the property and did not find any other prints leading from the house back out to the forest. He thought frantically then, perhaps an intruder was inside the house, someone who had come walking through the woods on this cold night. Andreas searched and searched in vain all over the house. But did not find any strange people on the premises, with nothing out of place or missing. Andreas Gruber settled down to uneasy sleep that night, still unable to figure out where the strange footsteps might have come from, and who had made them while entering his house.

Later that same night, Andreas was awoken by strange and unexplained noises coming from the attic. He remembered what their previous maid said about sounds and voices in the attic. Andreas decided then and there to check for himself who was making the strange noises, but he did not find anything in the attic. Andreas could barely fathom what was happening by that time. He felt that he could also be losing his mind. What were these odd noises and the strange footprints that he saw earlier, were they just in his head? It was as if an intruder had come in from the forest, entered their home, and simply disappeared into thin air.

The next morning, the strange occurrences continued with a vengeance. Andreas found a newspaper on his front porch that he had never seen before, and no one in his household recognized. Later that day, he walked by the tool shed out back and was confused to see multiple scratches and deep cuts on the door as if someone was trying to break into the shed. By that time, the strangeness of what was happening finally got to Andreas, and he talked with his nearest neighbors about the strange events happening in Hinterkaifeck. The neighbors also shared that Andreas casually mentioned to them that his own set of house keys recently went missing. Crestfallen, the neighbors recounted to the authorities after the massacre, that the loss of the keys coincidentally happened a few days before the tragedy that befell the Gruber household. Sadly, no one reported these incidents to the authorities before the savage attack on the unknowing family.

On the fateful and tragic day of March 31, 1922, a new maid named Maria Baumgartner (44) was on her way to the Gruber household to begin her first day of work. Maria would never know that while she cheerfully reported for work that day, in just a few hours of her stepping in the threshold of the cursed Hinterkaifeck farm. Maria would be savagely murdered for being in the wrong place at the worst possible time.

Four days after the fateful day, on April 4, the Gruber's absence was palpably felt and finally noticed in the nearby town, and the townspeople were starting to worry about the family and their new maid.

Viktoria's young daughter, Cäzilia, was not showing up for her classes at school, and Viktoria herself had not been attending Church, which was very unlike her. The postman in town also noticed that the Gruber's mail was unclaimed as well. Something was amiss; a few townsfolk decided to go to the Gruber's farm to check in on them and make sure they were safe. When the group of concerned citizens knocked on the Gruber's doors and called out for them, no one answered. A search of the property and by the nearby forest did not produce anything beyond the norm, either. The townsfolk also noted that the air in Hinterkaifeck farm on that terrible day was stale and eerily quiet.

The barn was the last building checked. The townspeople opened the door and met with the most horrific sight ever imagined. On the floor of the old barn, lying in a gruesome pool of their blood, lay the lifeless bodies of Andreas, his wife, his daughter Viktoria and his young granddaughter, Cäzilia. The bodies were positioned in the middle of the barn and covered in hay. The Gruber family appeared to have been systematically lured into the barn one by one and brutally attacked as they innocently entered to face their untimely death. As horrifying as the scene in the barn was, what was even more painfully apparent to those who were witnesses on that terrible day, was the sight of the dead little girl Cäzilia with clumps of her hair torn out of her scalp. They could only deduce that she had been alive long enough after the attack on her to witness the scene in the barn, straight from hell, that unfolded in front of her innocent eyes.

Upon discovering the bodies in the barn, the townsfolk began to search for the new maid frantically Maria and the little boy Josef, in case they were still alive and needed help. But they were tragically found in the farmhouse and suffered the same evil fate as the others, the little boy Josef lying on top of his bed in Viktoria's bedroom and the maid, Maria, was found dead in her bedroom. It was apparent that both the maid and the little boy had also lost enormous amounts of blood. On that fateful and tragic day, it was confirmed by all those present that all six members of the Hinterkaifeck Farm had been brutally murdered, in cold blood.

The townspeople immediately called the authorities, and a few hours later, police officers from the Munich Police Department arrived. Inspector Georg Reingruber was the leader of the team in charge of the murder investigation. The police team initially suspected that the real motive for the Hinterkaifeck murders was a robbery, and they proceeded to interrogate suspicious-looking people from the nearby villages, as well as transient merchants and even beggars in the vicinity. But that robbery theory was laid to rest when a significant sum of money was quickly discovered, in the house during the investigation, and all the other family valuables remained intact as well. A thief would have found that a large sum of money quickly and would have made off with all the family heirlooms if that was the real motive.

During the ongoing police investigation, authorities discovered that a few weeks before the hellish night at Hinterkaifeck, Viktoria completely emptied her bank account. She even borrowed some additional funds from her half-sister (Andreas Gruber was the senior Cäzilia's second husband) to serve as seed money for investing in their farmstead. Viktoria had also surreptitiously donated a 700 gold mark in the Church confessional. When the parish priest traced the sizeable amount back to her as the secret donor,

Viktoria told the priest to keep the money "for missionary work." During the investigation, the police did not know if it was related to the murders. But, the sizable withdrawal from Viktoria's bank account was never accounted for.

Another theory and criminal motive, the investigators played around with, was the possibility of the murders being a crime of passion. The police widely speculated that Viktoria's former ardent suitor, a man by the name of Lorenz Schlittenbauer, had a plausible motive to want the Gruber family dead. It was widely talked-about in town if Schlittenbauer could be young Josef's true father. The majority believed this was not so and that Josef was the product of an abusive relationship between Viktoria and her father, Andreas. When the police interrogated Schlittenbauer, he confessed that he knew about Andreas and Viktoria's illicit and illegal relationship and was disgusted by it. The motive was that this sordid incestuous relationship must have enraged the love-struck Schlittenbauer, and he retaliated by killing the entire family, even his alleged son, the young Josef. The police persisted in following up on this particular murder motive involving the suspect, but they were unable to find enough evidence to support this claim. The police leads were all turning up with dead ends and steadily started to grow cold.

A day after the horrible discovery of the murders in Hinterkaifeck, on April 5, 1922, the court physician, Dr. Johann Baptist Aumüller, performed all the medical autopsies in the barn of the farmstead. The physician established that a farm tool such as a *hatchet*, or German pickaxe, was the logical murder weapon. Each victim was killed the same way, with a single and forceful blow to the head. The way the murderer used the *hatchet* determined that, although the murderer was very precise, it only killed with one blow. But, there was a lot of hatred in each swing of the *hatchet*. Because the heads of the victim had all split open with the impact, but the bodies were untouched. Whoever the murderer was, they were very comfortable using the *hatchet*.

The autopsies showed that all the victims died instantly, except for the little girl and daughter of Viktoria, Cäzilia. The terrified little girl survived for several hours after the single blow to her head. It was unimaginable to think of what was going through Cäzilia's mind during those terrible hours. Whatever her thoughts were, they were horrifying enough to cause her to pull out tufts of her hair from her scalp while the life seeped out of her weak little body on the barn floor.

The police spent many days investigating the crime scene, concluding that an intruder must have figured out a way to lure Andreas, Cäzilia, her daughter Viktoria and young Cäzilia into the barn, one at a time, over a series of hours. Police thought the first two victims to be Viktoria and her mother, Cäzilia, because they were in there evening clothes, and their deaths were probably earlier in the evening than the rest. The killer then proceeded to the farmhouse to finish off the little boy Josef and maid Maria. The murder covered all of the bodies with some sort of material. The bodies in the barn were all covered with hay, Josefs mother's skirt covered him, and the bedsheet covered the maid Maria. This strange show of delayed courtesy and false modesty for the dead bodies points towards a theory that the killer had some sort of emotional bond or connection with the victims, and by covering them up, it would hide what the killer had done.

Another bizarre occurrence to add to an already convoluted murder mystery was what the neighbors witnessed on the weekend right after the murders. The date of death was determined to be March 31, and it was four days before anyone discovered the bodies at Hinterkaifeck. However, neighbors claimed to have seen smoke coming out of the chimney on the last two days. The animals on the farm were well-fed, the family dog was tied up in the barn unharmed with food and water. Nothing indicated the animals had gone almost a week without food. Police also found a bed in the farmhouse showing signs of recently being slept in, meaning that after murdering the victims, the killer stayed around for a few days. Unbothered by the covered corpses in the vicinity. The murderer possibly slept in the house, and even cooked food, as the neighbors claimed to see smoke from the chimney.

Throughout the years, the police have questioned 100 or so murder suspects and even employed clairvoyants to try and figure out what happened at Hinterkaifeck farm. If the murderer made the noises in the attic that the first maid heard before she left. That meant the killer would have been in the attic for over six months before the actual murder-spree. Then right after the brutal murders, the killer would have had the audacity to stay for almost a week, very much at home in the unfortunate Gruber household. The case has been continuously reopened in 1996, and most recently, in 2007. However, all the evidence always ended up leading to dead ends on a very cold case.

The farm was demolished the year after the tragedy, as the townsfolk did not want a remaining relic to remind them of the horrific events that took place in the spring of 1922. A monument was erected nearby, the only symbol of the gruesome and bloody murders that took place at the Hinterkaifeck Farm. Only the ancient trees are left standing in the old forest, the only things alive that played mute witness to what happened on that horrible and gruesome night.

2

CREEPY MYSTERIOUS WHISTLING

Whistler Haunts Fiancee Of Louisiana Trooper

NEW ORLEANS — (UP) — A persistent whistler is haunting Jacqueline Cadow, 19, the pretty, well-trailed fiancee of a Louisiana State Trooper.

I n 1950, in the small town of Paradis, Louisiana, a disturbing phantom presence lurked and preyed on one unlucky resident, causing her to lose her mind with anxiety and fear. Her name was Jacqueline Cadow, a teenager living a normal life in her small Louisiana town until the whistled eerie strains of a funeral march changed her way of life forever. The strange occurrences all began with one whistle, with a sound like a rude "cat call" used by cheeky boys wanting to get the attention of shapely ladies passing near them. But the catcall whistles were soon replaced by furtive whispers, disturbing phone calls, and the worst was when this escalated to strange whistled music, morbidly heard in only funeral services and marches. These sounds terrorized poor Jacqueline constantly. She even listened to the whistles from the supposed privacy and safety of her bedroom window at night. But try as she did, Jacqueline could never catch a glimpse of the Phantom Whistler that seemed to stalk her every move. Sadly, because Jacqueline was only a teenager at 18 years old, most people did not believe her Phantom Whistler stalker stories; some folks even said that she was just doing this to attract attention.

Jacqueline started to become very frightened, especially with the strange noises coming from right outside her bedroom window. She would call the police to go to their home to investigate her claims of the Phantom Whistler stalking her. But, the police could never find any suspicious individuals close to the Cadow home whenever they responded to her calls for help. Jacqueline's claims seemed false and possibly existed only in her wild imagination. It was like the Boy Who Cried Wolf, the authorities deduced, and they stopped coming over when Jacqueline called for help time and time again.

That all changed when one day, it was Jacqueline's mother who heard the eerie and disembodied whistling sounds. She described to the police that the sinister sound seemed to be coming right from the window of Jacqueline's room. The cops came over again and investigated the claims from the new witness because this time, another person corroborated Jacqueline's mysterious Phantom Whistler story. But just like before, the police could not pin down any suspects as no one around the vicinity could have made any menacing whistling sounds. There was nothing that the police could do, and so they left. But the whistling noises continued to haunt Jacqueline every day.

The Whistler would start by whistling funeral songs: eerie and somber music, right outside her window, which would then be accompanied by low moans and wails. Jacqueline did her best to continue with her life, despite her strange troubles at home. And through all this mysterious and turbulent state of affairs, Jacqueline was still able to find love, and she got engaged to her fiancé, State Trooper Herbert Belsom. As a man of the law, Belsom also investigated the Phantom Whistler in his official capacity. But he had no luck with this, just like all the police investigations in the past.

Jacqueline's engagement to State Trooper Belsom enraged her mysterious Phantom Whistler suitor. The whistle harassment escalated menacingly, with the Whistler calling Jacqueline on the phone, first making strange comments about her fiancé's mustache and then horribly moaning into the phone receiver. The Whistler then pushed his danger-ously bizarre behavior even more by threatening Jacqueline and members of her family, saying he would stab them several times, cut her throat, and made other various threats to her life. All because she got engaged, and if the Phantom Whistler could not have Jacqueline to himself, he would make sure that no one would enjoy that same pleasure. He repeatedly told Jacqueline not to marry her fiancé because if she did, he would kill her and her brother too. For months, the phone call threats went on, and eventually, Jacqueline would just hear funeral music being whistled from outside her window, followed by blood-curdling screams.

Jacqueline decided that, for her safety and her family's as well, she would move around, staying at different friends and family member's houses to get away from the Phantom Whistler. The situation had gotten so much more severe, and the police got involved again.

Unfortunately, Jacqueline's ploy of moving around did not work, and the Whistler followed her from house to house, including her aunt's house and that of a concerned friend's home, who she barely even knew. Every time, the Whistler found her and continued to terrorize her.

The local newspaper soon caught wind of what was happening to Jacqueline Cadow and started covering the story. There were many newspaper stories at the time, covering the strange Phantom Whistler and how his menacing whistling and stalking of Jacqueline were slowly driving her mad. Newspaper reporters came out to inter-view Jacqueline and witnessed the phone calls and the whistling outside her bedroom window. When they went outside to find who was whistling, there was no one there.

Many family members living in the home with Jacqueline, including her mother and father, heard the whistling and moaning. Witnesses to the sounds claimed the sounds were not those that a human would make, but instead, it sounded disembodied and otherworldly, almost like a supernatural being from the unknown. On several occasions, men who were witness to the noises while they were standing outside Jacqueline's bedroom window, immediately undertook a quick search for the culprit but, never catching anyone.

Jacqueline suffered a collapse and fainting spell one day when she, her mother, her aunt, and a New Orleans State newspaper reporter were all witnesses to another impending Whistler attack. State Police and the local authorities continued with their thorough investigation but found no suspect. Jacqueline, by that time, seemed to be at the end of her rope, so she went to stay at the house of her future in-law's, Herbert Belsom's parents. But still, the Whistler was able to trace her, and Jacqueline's mother received a call with an ominous voice rasping out on the telephone line: "Tell Jackie I know she's at Herbert's house."

Eventually, Jacqueline decided that she was going to have to move on with her life and marry the man that she loved and was engaged to. She couldn't continue living in fear and keep hiding all her life. On Jacqueline's wedding day, with hordes of local press and reporters covering the event, anticipating that the Phantom Whistler would make his final move on this big day in Jacqueline's life, nothing happened. Suddenly, as if he never existed, the Whistler vanished, the calls and the noises stopped. And Jacqueline never heard from the Phantom Whistler ever again.

The sheriff's department in the small town was embarrassed by the lack of evidence and not finding the culprit of these awful and menacing threats the whole time that they were on top of the investigation.

After the calls had stopped, the police released a statement claiming that the "phantom" was a "hoax," and it was "an inside job." The family was furious, and immediately, the police department recanted their statement. Later, the sheriff's department claimed that they had solved the case and caught the Whistler, but did not want to release the name of any other information, for fear of embarrassing the families involved.

However, when reporters and investigators tried to find arrest reports or any indication that the Whistler had been located and apprehended by the authorities, no records were showing any arrests.

No one knows who the Whistler was If he was indeed something from another world or just a sociopath who was very good at covering his tracks and being able to evade witnesses and the police. Was this all a simple game for the Whistler or, indeed, just a maniac obsessively in love with a girl who would never love him back? These are questions lost in the wind, but perhaps one day, alone, the eerie whistle will once again break the silence of the night to menace yet another innocent victim like Jacqueline Cadow.

3

THE HOUSE THAT BLEEDS

On September 8, 1987, Mr. and Mrs. Winston discovered that a large amount of blood had suddenly appeared in four out of the six rooms of their house. This phenomenon started just when Mrs. Minnie

Winston was stepping out of her bath that night. She was shocked to see blood all over the bathroom floor. She and her husband William were both just under 80 years old, so it was automatic for her to panic, thinking that her husband might be gravely injured. Upon checking up on him, Mrs. Winston found William quite well and not bleeding.

They walked throughout the house in stunned amazement, seeing blood splattered everywhere. They were finding pools of blood in the kitchen, the living room, and the bedroom. There was blood on the walls, under some of their appliances, and even in the basement. The Winstons began cleaning up the blood as best as they could, despite the volume and proceeded to call the police. The Atlanta Police Department investigated the incident. The police described the scene as soaked with "copious amounts of blood." The blood was collected and tested by the crime lab to determine the blood type, which ended up being O-positive. Neither Mr. nor Mrs. Winston's blood type was O-positive. The blood had not come from them.

The police continued the investigation going through all the possible scenarios. Did they have guests recently? No, they did not. Did they have any animals in the house? There were no pets in the house. While Mr. Winston's health regimen included dialysis at home, the blood was already confirmed to not belong to either of them. Everyone was at a complete loss. The nation picked the story up. It showed up on talk shows, news reports, and newspapers around the states. People all over the country were speculating about the cause of this bloody occurrence. Theories flew, and imaginations soared. All sorts of ideas came up. Was it an elaborate hoax? Or was it demonic manifestations?

Further investigations revealed, interestingly, that the blood splatter found in the house were of different patterns. There was blood sprayed in areas, as if it came from a spray bottle, while in other areas, it looked as if it was spilled or dumped. There were small droplets of blood and large streaks on the walls. The areas that appeared sprayed suggested a spray bottle (or wherever the blood came from) was pointing in a downward direction. In some instances, the spattered blood was many feet above the floor, indicating height.

While police analyzed the home like a crime scene, they did conclude that they did not believe Mr. And Mrs. Winston were suspects of any crime that occurred in their home.

Sometime later, a private investigator, acting on his interest in the case, decided to contact Winston's and interviewed with them to perhaps get to the bottom of this mystery. The P.I. also contacted the police only to find out that the case was closed in less than six months, and the detective that was the original investigator was not with the police department anymore.

The private investigator discovered this much. While Winston's are a pleasant couple, they, however, were very apprehensive about discussing the occurrence of the blood that appeared on the walls of their home. Mrs. Winston stated that she and her husband lived there for 22 years and had never experienced any strange incidents until then and became agitated when talking about it. Mrs. Winston claimed it was not, in fact, blood that manifested, but rather, rust and mud mixed with water that came from a burst pipe. She did not seem swayed by the fact that the evidence had been thoroughly tested by the police and confirmed by the crime lab to be blood.

Mrs. Winston said that if it had indeed been blood, then she would not have been able to continue to stay in the house. Therefore, it could not possibly be blood. Further, she denied any strange occurrences to have ever happened in the house. In contrast, she and her husband had lived there, thus ignoring any questions about the home, possibly being the site of some kind of supernatural power.

There were known facts of the Winston family that suggested a possible motive for committing a hoax of this nature. Winston's had access to blood because of Mr. Winston's kidney dialysis treatments. Likewise, Winston's daughter had access to blood as well, due to her working in a hospital. There was a rumor that their children staged the hoax to have Mr. and Mrs. Winston declared incompetent for financial reasons.

Another theory was the older couple staged the event to generate attention.

Whatever the speculation, Winston's continued to deny that the occurrence was a hoax up until their death. Although this was an alarming and unique case, this isn't the first bleeding house documentation in our world's history, and it certainly won't be our last.

4

THE CREEPY CURSE OF L.A.'S HOTEL CECIL

E lisa Lam was a 21-year-old Canadian student that traveled to downtown Los Angeles, and on February 19, 2013, was found dead inside the water tank of the Hotel Cecil.

She came to Los Angeles for a trip she dubbed a "West Coast

Tour" looking to explore the coast of California, including San Diego, Los Angeles, Santa Cruz, and San Francisco. Elisa was traveling alone, primarily on public transportation. She had already visited San Diego before she made her way up to Los Angeles, where, after two days, she checked into the Hotel Cecil, a hotel originally built in the 1920s.

The Hotel Cecil initially built as a business hotel that fell on hard economic times during the Depression and continued to decay. Located in the area of Los Angeles now dubbed "Skid Row," the hotel was widely associated with famous and controversial crimes in the 20th century. Among them is the 1947 gruesome case of Elizabeth Short - nicknamed by the press as the Black Dahlia, possibly about the mid-1946 dark movie 'The Blue Dahlia' - who was found with her body cut in half at the waist and drained of blood. Rumored, to bet last spotted at the Hotel Cecil. Also, in 1964, Goldie Osgood -known as the Pigeon Lady because she, well, loved to feed pigeons – was found raped and murdered in her room on the 7th floor of the same hotel. Several serial killers, such as Richard Ramirez (aka The Night Stalker) and Jack Unter-weger (aka The Vienna Strangler), both resided at the hotel during their killing sprees. Not to mention the many docu-mented suicides that took place there.

Elisa documented her travels on a blog she named "Ether Fields," which she began in mid-2010. In addition to travel-ing, she posted online about fashion and her recent bipolar diagnosis. Her family did not speak about her condition often and tended to deny the existence of the disorder. Elisa seemingly struggled with her illness and sought a forum to discuss her journey. She was supposedly taking mood-stabilizing drugs such as Wellbutrin, Lamictal, Seroquel, and Effexor, and may have inclined to suicidal tendencies. One report states that she had previously gone missing before her stay at the Hotel Cecil.

In January 2012, she posted on her blog that due to a recent relapse, she was taking the semester off at school to travel to the West Coast. When she set off on her trip, she made sure to keep in touch with her parents daily.

Because she was traveling alone, and due to her bi-polar disorder, she wanted to make sure her parents knew where she was at all times. On January 31, 2013, Elisa was due to check out of the Cecil and continue her trip to Santa Cruz. However, that day her parents did not hear from her; they immediately called the Los Angeles Police to report her disappearance. After speaking with the police, Elisa's parents boarded the next plane to Los Angeles.

The hotel staff had seen her that day, stating she was alone, while a local bookstore owner disclosed that she had seen Elisa earlier in the day in her store. The proprietor of the bookstore said Elisa was outgoing and "lively" and dropped by the bookstore to buy gifts to take home for her family. No one in the hotel had seen her with another person.

The police searched Elisa's hotel room and brought dogs to

explore the hotel for Elisa's scent. However, they were not able to find her. Police were unable to search every room of the hotel because they did not possess "probable cause" that a crime had occurred.

After a week of searching, the police took the case nationally, posting her picture around neighborhoods and businesses, in newspapers and online. The media found out about the mysterious disappearance, and suddenly, Elisa Lam's disappearance was a national concern.

By February 14, 2013, two weeks after Elisa's disappearance, the Los Angeles police department released a video of Elisa's last sighting in the hotel. In the video, Elisa is getting into the elevator of the hotel and manifesting curious, if not bizarre, behavior. This behavior is what got investigators and the public perplexed, leading to the proposition of numerous theories regarding her disappearance.

The video was a two-and-a-half-minute security camera clip, offering a fixed view of the inside of the elevator and the hallways right in front of where the elevator doors open. As can be seen, Elisa first enters the elevator, wearing a red hoodie sweatshirt and a gray t-shirt, then pushes buttons for several different floors and proceeds to stand against the elevator wall. When the doors fail to close, Elisa pops her head out of the elevator and looks outside into the hallway, then steps back into the elevator. She repeats this several times and then goes back to the control panel, pressing several more buttons, some more than once. She then places both hands over her ears and walks to the wall right outside the elevator cab and leans against the wall; the elevator doors are still open. Elisa then starts to rub her forearms together, waving her hands and bowing slightly forward while rocking. She is still in the hallway right in front of the elevator entrance, while the doors remain open. Elisa backs away to the wall again, turns to her left, and walks out of the camera's frame. After she walks away, the elevator doors finally close.

People repeatedly watched the video, causing speculation as to what Elisa was experiencing. In the video's first ten days on a social media site, the video received three million views and 40,000 comments. Some viewers stated she is possessed, while others thought she was playing the "Elevator Game," which is supposed to help you travel to another dimension. Some reasoned she was simply trying to get the elevator to move because someone was pursuing her. At the same time, a body language expert stated that she appeared to be under the influence of the drug Ecstasy or some other kind of party drug.

After the media discovered the truth about her mental disorder, many jumped to the conclusion that Elisa was having a mental breakdown and was unaware of her surroundings.

While police and Elisa's parents continued their search for her, guests of the Cecil began complaining to the hotel management and staff of weak water pressure in their rooms. Other guests of the hotel stated that their water was a strange color and had a terrible odor to it. Hotel employees went up to the roof to inspect the water tanks that pumped the city's water supply to the hotel. On that fateful February day, inside one of the tanks, the body of Elisa Lam was found floating face-up, just a foot below the water's surface.

Many of the guests immediately checked out, repulsed by the fact they had been drinking water that had a decomposing body floating in it for the last two and a half weeks. The Fire department drained the tanks within hours, and by noon of February 19, they discovered Elisa's body, her body pulled out of the tank where she floated, for two weeks. The entire water system had to be drained, refilled, and drained again before the city's health department allowed the hotel to use their water tanks. A long term resident made an unusual comment to police that day, stating that one of the upper-level rooms of the hotel had flooded right after Elisa's disappearance.

The medical examiner took Elisa's body and performed an autopsy. Two days after finding her body, the medical examiner stated her cause of death was drowning, with a major contributing factor being her bipolar disorder.

The medical report also stated that Elisa's body was found completely naked, with her clothes floating next to her body in the water tank. Police also discovered her hotel keys and wristwatch floating in the tank. The clothes found in the tank were the same clothes Elisa was wearing in the hotel elevator video- her red hoodie and a gray t-shirt. The medical examiner also mentioned finding a strange "sand-like particulate covering her clothes.

The examiner also concluded there were no signs of physical trauma. Additionally, neither the police nor the medical examiners found any evidence to suggest that Elisa had committed suicide. Toxicology tests were negative for any kind of illegal or recreational drug, but they did show she was taking her bi-polar prescription medications.

Although medical examiners and the police were able to state a cause of death for Elisa, they could not explain how she died. An even more mysterious fact was that the water tank, where they found Elisa's body, is located on top of the hotel's roof, with doors and stairs that were always locked and not easily accessed even by the hotel staff. If the doors and stairways had been forced open, an alarm would have sounded. The only way up to the roof, aside from the doors and stairs, was by taking the fire escape, which would have bypassed any alarms or locked doors. The fire escape was obscure, so Elisa would have had to know it was there or have been with someone who knew it was there.

In addition to the difficulty Elisa faced to get to the roof, the other issue involved the height of the water tanks.

Many investigators believe that the water tanks were too tall for Elisa to get into by herself. The hotel staff had to use a ladder just to look inside the container. The water tanks were cement cylinders that rose five feet tall, and there was no place, no ladder, and no stool, from where she could have anchored her feet to hoist herself up and over.

Till this day, questions and propositions continue to linger. Some people believe that she was high on a cocktail of drugs that went undetected, as it may have broken down in her bloodstream due to the time and condition of her body. The medical examiners were also not entirely convinced that Elisa's death was merely an accident. In their report, they mention evidence of subcutaneous pooling of blood in her anus, which could suggest sexual abuse. However, this may be because of the bloating of her body, suspended in the tank for an extended period.

Perhaps one of the most bizarre facts of this case was Elisa's social media account on "Tumblr." Elisa's phone was never found and could be presumed lost or stolen around the time of her death. However, posts made to the social media account after she already died. Many explain this could be a function performed on Tumblr that allows a user to "schedule" posts, suggesting that she created the Tumblr posts in advance. Others, though, have speculated that they are posts from her killer.

Elisa's death continues to be a mystery. Meanwhile, the Hotel Cecil is still open and serving guests, although its name has changed since the latter part of 2014. It is now named "Stay on Main." However, the original building that once went by the name Hotel Cecil is still open for business and more mysterious occurrences.

5

FAMILY PHONE-STALKER MYSTERY

In 2007, an individual that called himself the "Phone Stalker" began terrorizing the Kuykendall family as well as several other families located in Washington State. The families claimed that they felt they were in a real-life horror movie. The calls began randomly, and no one can explain how or why they started.

This story started in February 2007, when Courtney Kuykendall's cell phone started sending text messages by itself, without the aid of Courtney. These text messages received by her friends and family members and were, at first, harmless. Soon after mysteriously sending the text messages, the scary phone calls started. A scratchy voice on the other end of the line would come on and claim that he was going to slit her entire family's throats. These calls were happening every day, and stumping the Kuykendall's and the police. No one knew where they were coming from. A trace on the calls led them right back to the Kuykendall's phones.

After that, the Phone Stalker intensified his efforts to terrorize the Kuykendall family, as well as two other families in the Washington state area. One theory proposed that the stalker was able to hack into the family member's phones and spy on them. The hackers knew what the families were doing, what they were wearing, and where they were.

The Phone Stalker even started recording private conversations, while *turned off* and then sent those to the families.

If any member of the families did not answer the phone, the stalker would simply leave a message. In one of the voice messages played for ABC News, the stalker states, "I know where you are. I know where you live. I'm going to kill you." The stalker was also able to change settings on the phones, including switching them on, modifying ring tones and volume control. Even scarier, the stalker stated that he knew when the kids left for school in the morning and when they were alone and unattended.

After that, the Kuykendall's installed a new security system. However, Mrs. Kuykendall received a call stating that he knew the new security code. One day, while Mrs. Kuykendall was slicing oranges in her kitchen, her phone rang, and the voice on the other end of the phone stated, "I prefer lemons."

The Kuykendalls contacted the police, hoping they would be able to help. But then, the Kuykendall's started receiving calls threatening them and telling them not to talk to the police. The family also received the recorded conversation that they recently had with the actual police detective. It came to the point that a day without a call from the 'Phone Stalker' was a good day.

Police were utterly stumped, unable to trace the calls back to anyone outside of the families. Most of the calls directed at Courtney Kuykendall traced back to her phone. Although the police never considered Courtney suspect, many members of the community believed this to be a desperate cry for attention from the teenaged girl.

Even after the family changed phones and phone numbers twice, the calls were still coming through, possibly indicated that whoever was behind the heinous calls had physical access to the phones to install the hacking software.

Whether it was a family member, an obsessed stalker, or even a supernatural being, its intent was to terrorizing Courtney and the other families. The 'Phone Stalker' has never been caught, was unable to be traced, and may very well still be out there, just biding the time until the next victim.

6

MORE THAN A TOY

Most people consider Ouija boards to be little more than an exotic means of passing the time or frightening a jumpy friend during a slumber party. Ouija boards are often bought as a plaything and perceived as toys that a few folks will even gift to their children without any second thought.

Despite all of this dismissal, others are terrified of this medium and believe firmly that Ouija boards are not a toy. It is a common belief that those who so carelessly attempt to contact the world beyond for personal amusement can easily find themselves amid a horrifying maelstrom of unholy happenings, such as continuous haunting by an unseen force or even possession. Whatever your feelings are concerning the board, there have been several stories and personal accounts that have cropped up over the years about things going awry and ending up as anything but fun.

Bizarre experiences with Ouija boards have frequently been a part of many famous paranormal stories involving hauntings and possessions in the past. But, there have also been a plethora of accounts all over the Internet in recent years. People from all walks of life have got more than they bargained for by merely letting their morbid curiosity get the best of them. Reddit is a true testament of this with its countless user-submitted stories on the subject, told by people who learned not to take the issue lightly, but who learned the hard way. More striking, however, are probably tales from the past, which have embedded themselves deeply in popular culture and lore.

Perhaps one of the best-known cases is that of the unfortunate Maryland boy. Investigators gave him the name Roland Doe to protect his identity after the horrific events that transpired in the late 1940s. This incident would later go on to inspire the novel entitled "The Exorcist," as well as the famous movie of the same title. Roland was only fourteen at the time when his aunt introduced him to the Ouija board. The boy spent a lot of time playing with his aunt, and he harbored peculiar interests, such as dabbling in the paranormal. His aunt herself was involved in exploring and practicing similar things, too, while the boy's parents were known as very religious folks.

Things took a horrifying turn after Roland's aunt passed away in early 1949, leaving the boy grief-stricken and lonely. As the story goes, Roland decided to attempt to contact his aunt using the Ouija board. At that point, bizarre occurrences started to befall Roland and his family, with most of the paranormal activity following wherever Roland would go. Several authors and journalists documented the details of these events and those involved, including Thomas B. Allen.

The family soon began to experience unsettling sounds and sights around their homes, such as marching and other strange noises and household items and furniture moving without visible interference from anybody. Some sources also stated that these unexplained happenings weren't limited to just the home but appeared to follow Roland outside when he went to school. Other times, objects would levitate or be thrown across the room anywhere in the proximity of Roland.

The boy's parents sought medical and psychiatric advice to

contain their son's strange behavior, which grew increasingly menacing and dark. It wasn't long until the couple decided to seek the assistance of their family pastor. They all agreed that Roland should spend a night at the pastor's house for further observation and evaluation, as the priest wanted to make sure that demonic influence was real.

Sure enough, the pastor got his confirmation very quickly when strange sounds started to occur in the night, such as loud scratching and rattling from Roland's bed. The pastor also reported that objects and furniture around his home would move of their own accord. Whether or not the Lutheran pastor was utterly realistic in his assessments, he quickly advised the family to turn to a Catholic priest for further help, seemingly feeling overwhelmed.

Soon after that, the case landed in the hands of a Catholic priest by the name of Edward Hughes. This man decided to perform an exorcism on Roland, which was to take place at a Jesuit institution of Georgetown University Hospital. The priest restrained Roland to a bed for the ritual, but it quickly became apparent that the boy possessed an almost super-human strength when he managed to free one of his hands after a beastly struggle. Roland then allegedly tore out spring from the mattress and attacked the priest with it, inflicting a severe laceration on his arm in the process.

This injury forced Hughes to cease the exorcism ritual for the time being, and the family took the afflicted boy home that same night. It was then, according to the family members, that things started to get even more bewildering. Namely, they reported that the words "Saint Louis" materialized on the boy's chest, written in blood. This experience is what led the family to take Roland to Saint Louis and seek further assistance from the Catholic clergy.

Their relatives in Saint Louis established contact with two more priests, Raymond J. Bishop and William S. Bowdern, who agreed to visit Roland in their home and assess the situation. Sure enough, the priests observed more of what the others had seen thus far. Roland's bed was vibrating and shaking from an invisible force, objects launched around the room, the boy spoke in a terrifying voice, and he appeared to harbor a deep disgust for any religious symbols. These actions quickly convinced the two priests that a demon was at work and had taken possession of the poor boy.

Right after that, the priests sought and received permission from their archbishop to perform an exorcism on Roland at the Alexian Brothers Hospital in Saint Louis, where Walter Halloran, another Catholic priest, joined them. The number of witnesses grew, and intense exorcism rituals began to take place over the next two months.

What transpired during these exorcisms was recorded in the diaries of the priests. But a lot of what is known also came from Halloran's numerous statements and testimonies. Reportedly, the boy showed demonic defiance to the many exorcising attempts by the priests. He would spit and shout abuse in a hellish voice at those present. His bed was said to have shaken violently, and Halloran also testified to the boy breaking his nose at one point. Perhaps most shockingly, though, Halloran also said of words appearing on the boy's body, such as "hell." Bishop's diary also made mention of brandings and mysterious scratches looking all over Roland.

After around thirty attempts altogether, it was said by those involved that the priests finally banished the demon from Roland and that he went on to live a life as usual as one could expect from those afflicted by such horror.

There have been details lost of the event due to how long ago the incident took place and diluting of facts by word of mouth over time. But the most crucial point of the experience has endured to this day. Because the teenager's identity was protected, we can't know much about what became of him other than what was told by those involved, but one can hope that Roland Doe went on to never play with the board again. Local records of the rituals are scarce, and the hospital in Saint Louis would later be demolished.

Whatever the details of those days may be and however reliable the accounts, stories like this are numerous enough to make anyone wary of this supposed toy. Some people have established contact with the other side through an Ouija board where everything would end as soon as the ritual was over, letting them go merrily about their business. However, sometimes, whatever is summoned may not feel like going back to its realm and may want to go home with you.

7

CREEPIEST TRUE STORIES FROM REDDITOR

Historic, high-profile tales and legends that have left a mark upon the popular culture are fascinating in their own right. But, sometimes, the terrifying stories of horror and macabre can be found on forums. One such forum where people gather to share all sorts of exciting stories and information is undoubtedly Reddit. Across its many "subreddits," users have shared quite a few terrifying, personal horror stories over the years. Some of which concern unexplained or paranormal events, while others are terrifying in a very natural way, primarily due to the high possibility of them being real. We'll take a look at a couple of the scariest tales one can find.

A slightly creepy tale was submitted by a user who claimed to have worked as an emergency services 911 operator. One day, he received a call from an older lady who sought assistance because she was feeling ill. The operator gathered the necessary information and then tried his best to keep the woman on the line to make sure she didn't collapse before the ambulance arrived. Still, the woman kept insisting that she had to go to the bathroom but promised to leave the door to her house unlocked for the ambulance.

Finally, the elderly lady put the phone down and went away, leaving the operator guessing. Soon enough, the ambulance arrived, and things took a turn for the peculiar. The EMTs at the scene got back in contact with the operator, asking all kinds of strange questions. They wanted to know if the operator was sure beyond any doubt that it was the lady who called requesting assistance explicitly for her self.

The operator was sure but was shocked to hear that they confirmed the woman was in the bathroom and had been dead for around twelve hours. The incident left this Reddit user perplexed, wondering to this day if someone else had been in the house or if he had received a call from a dead woman.

While this person was far away and safe from any mysterious circumstances, our next storyteller didn't have the same luck. Around three years ago, this user-submitted a story of her encounter with horror that was all too real and human.

Creepy Shadow

As this Redditers story goes, she was only a small child of around four or five years of age at the time. Her parents were, separated at that point, so she spent time with both her parents and was, on this particular occasion, staying in her mother's apartment. On that warm summer night, the girl was sleeping with her mother with an open window over the bed.

When she suddenly woke up in the middle of the night, she met with the unusual sight of their pet cat sitting in the door frame of her mother's room, apparently on alert. The poster noted that this was strange because the cat usually slept with them in the bed through the night. Through the open door, the girl could see her room just across the narrow hallway. At that moment, the cat walked over and went into the little girl's room, starting to meow.

The girl turned to her mother to wake her up, and, after only a couple of seconds, they both looked over through the door only to see an unusual man leaving the girl's bedroom. Her mother reacted immediately by throwing the girl out of the window, which wasn't high up on this first-floor apartment. After they both made their way out of the window, the police were called to the scene by neighbors.

The police found no signs of forced entry. The front door was unlocked, despite the girl's mother being sure she locked it. A week later, her mother found a notebook with drawings and names on it, along with a pair of gloves and a few gum wrappers in the kitchen. Her mother notified the police of these new findings. The police concluded that the man had probably made his way into the apartment before their bedtime, waiting until they fell asleep to come out of his hiding place and stalk the premises.

Someone's Knocking.

Three years ago, a Reddit user, who no longer has an account, told a story of a horrifying crime that marked his life when he was only twelve years old. As the short story went, he was but a ten-year-old boy at the time when he moved to live with his father in a neighborhood where he had no friends. The only acquaintances were a family who was friends of his dad. This family consisted of one single mother and her three children, one of whom was a twelve-year-old girl who befriended the boy over the next couple of years.

They weren't particularly close, but they kept the same company and often hung out together with other kids. One night, the Redditt user's friend named Rob was with the girl and her younger brother, hanging out at the girl's house. The kids were alone in the house with the girl's mother still at work. When they heard a knock on the door, they assumed it was the girl's mother coming home from work. At that point, Rob left through the window because he wasn't allowed to hang around so late. The girl, without a second thought, opened the door.

Sadly, it wasn't the girl's mother who had knocked, but the mentally deranged sister of the woman her mother worked with, recently released from an institution. She found out, from talking to her sister, where the single mother lived with her kids. She mapped out the woman's work schedule, knowing full well when the children would be home alone.

The girl's younger brother ran away to call the police from a neighbor's house, as the insane woman proceeded to murder the girl in her home brutally. The original poster stated that he didn't know too many details, except for what he heard later on, and the few details he did hear were bone-chilling. The crazed woman decapitated the poor girl, left her naked body on display, and hid her head, which was only found later by the police.

What's also shocking is that the same Redditt user returned only a while afterward to the same thread, posting links that he had found concerning his story. These articles confirmed the victim as being a fourteen-year-old girl named Adrienne Amikons. Viciously slain by a forty-year-old Jean Anne

Rudski, who was subsequently charged, tried, and committed to a mental institution on the grounds of being mentally unstable to bear legal responsibility. The horrific crime took place in Ontario in 1997.

The girl's decapitated body was left in a bloody bathtub for police to find upon inspecting the house. Police found the suspect covered in blood, holding a knife, just outside of the home, where police tackled her to the ground, injuring one officer lightly by the blade.

Between the official story and the one posted by the Reddit user, the only significant discrepancy seems to be that the official accounts stated the murder as having happened at Jean Anne's own house. This fact can be explained by it being an old event from childhood that most people would probably suppress in their conscience.

Whether or not the Reddit user was a friend of the murdered girl, verifies the story as having taken place, which adds a whole new level of eeriness to the countless other tales of horror and macabre you can find on Reddit.

8

MURDER CASTLE

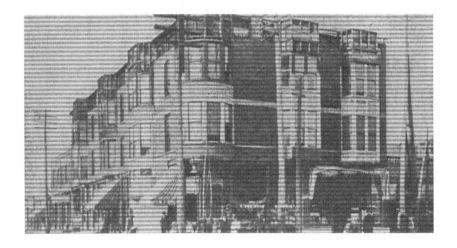

Now this story focuses on one particular individual who was very unstable, disturbed, and possibly inflicted with some kind of terrible mental illness, compelling him to kill. Mr. Holmes is known as America's very first serial killer documented, believed to have killed upwards of 200 people. We are not talking about a mass murderer wherein the instruments for murder were a bomb or anything that would cause massive destruction. The idea of using and killing anyone to deploy his various illegal moneymaking scams and schemes would consume him.

The site where Mr. Holmes committed most of the heinous murders was at his hotel that he erected in 1893, around the time of the World Columbian Exposition. The blueprints, made to Mr. Holmes' explicit specifications, included plenty of rooms and chambers for his manic, murderous mind.

Dr. Henry Howard Holmes was born as Herman W. Mudgett in 1861 in New Hampshire. He changed his name soon after, and although he regularly got into juvenile trouble, he was excellent as a student. Unfortunately, his father was a violent alcoholic, which may have predisposed Holmes to the ways of torture and killing. Holmes was incredibly intelligent and was the brunt of many a bully's attempts to punish him for his top grades in every class. On one of these occasions, Holmes was forced into a doctor's office and made to stand face-to-face with a real human skeleton. "At first, I was terrified," Holmes would later recount. However, he took the skull in his hands and suddenly felt exhilarated and fascinated.

He soon picked up the hobby of dissecting animals, and the first stirrings of his obsession with death emerged.

Holmes graduated early from high school, was married and

had a son. He eventually became a certified public accountant and once served as a city manager.

It was not surprising how well he did in his personal and business life; he was friendly and gregarious; everyone liked him. He then attended medical school at the University of Michigan. While enrolled, Holmes would take the corpses from the school's hospital, disfigure them, take insurance policies on them, and claim to insurance companies that the individuals were killed in a car accident. Soon after graduating, he left his wife and son one day, never to return.

Holmes then traveled throughout the country, stopping in Pennsylvania long enough to meet a young girl and marry her, although he had never finalized the divorce with his first wife. He then had another child, a girl this time.

Holmes arrived in Chicago shortly after and ventured at several businesses before ending up working for a local pharmacy. He had gotten along quite well with the owner, Mrs. Holton, and was very diligent. After some time, Holmes allegedly asked Mrs. Holton if he could purchase the store to which, he claimed, she reportedly agreed to. When people in the neighborhood asked where the original owner was, Holmes stated she had moved to California. But she was never seen again.

It was in a vacant lot across the pharmacy where Holmes' "Murder Castle" would be built - it was called "The World's Fair Hotel."

It was an entire block long and three stories high. The bottom level contained commercial shops and Holmes' newly relocated pharmacy. In the top two floors, Holmes' office and living quarters were found, along with a "labyrinth" of rooms. Some of the doorways led to brick walls, and many were strangely angled. Building stairs that went nowhere, constructing several doors that only opened from the outside of the rooms. Holmes continuously fired workers and then re-hired new ones; he wanted to make sure that he was the only person who knew the actual layout and design of the building.

Many of his victims began with the employees of the hotel, whom Holmes required to carry life insurance policies that he paid for, but he always ensured that he, too, was their sole beneficiary. Holmes also killed guests and many girlfriends within the various rooms of the hotel. Sometimes Holmes would take women to an entirely soundproof room and pump deadly gas into it. Watching the victims asphyxiate. Another place was named "the hanging room," where he would lead his victims and hang them alive and watch them die. One room made entirely of brick was accessible by a trap door in the ceiling and was used to starve victims to death.

To dispose of the bodies, Holmes created various ways within the hotel to accomplish this task. Sometimes he would use a metal shoot that went to a secret compartment in the basement; there was a dummy elevator as well that descended into the basement. In the cellar, Holmes would dissect the bodies, stage them, strip the flesh, and sometimes sell them to medical schools. There were also two giant furnaces created where he was able to burn the bodies and the evidence of their deaths.

One of his victims was also his lover, named Julia Smythe. She worked at the jewelry counter at his pharmacy and was married at the time the affair with Holmes began. Smythe's husband learned of the relationship and left her and their daughter Pearl, and never returned. Smythe became pregnant while she was with Holmes and demanded marriage from him. Holmes, not wanting a child, said that he would marry her, only if she received an abortion. On Christmas Eve, the night the abortion was to be performed, Holmes killed Smythe by overdosing her with chloroform and then killed her daughter.

Holmes kept her body and employed a local criminal that he had worked with before to help Holmes articulate the body. They chopped off her arms, and the accomplice proceeded to ready the limbs for medical schools while Holmes worked on the body at the hotel. Holmes had the man working with him transport Symthe's body in two sections to get her out of the hotel. Then taking her body to a house, where two other dead bodies would arrive shortly after. When the police finally caught Holmes, they would call this house "the house of three corpses."

After police captured Holmes, years later, and with many

miles traveled throughout the United States in the search for him, his trial began in October 1885. Holmes claimed at the hearing:

"I was born with the devil in me. I could not help the fact that I was a murderer, no more than the poet can help the inspiration to sing – I was born with the "Evil One" standing as my sponsor beside the bed where I was ushered into the world, and he has been with me since."

-H.H. Holmes

Holmes confessed to 30 murders. However, there were so many bodies found; the number is closer to 200. An executioner hung Holmes at the Philadelphia State Prison in 1896. However, just previous to Holmes' hanging, Murder Castle was mysteriously set on fire and destroyed in 1938.

Years later, after Holmes' death, the original caretaker of "Murder Castle" was found dead in his home; he had committed suicide by swallowing strychnine. investigators discovered his body with a note that simply stated: "I couldn't sleep." Several months before his death, family members of the caretaker said that he claimed to be "haunted" but would not say by whom.

His family also reported that he had hallucinations and was bordering on a psychotic break.

Holmes believed certain people were doomed from birth, born with the devil inside of them. Once possessed, it was impossible to keep the urges to kill at bay. Many serial killers, past and present, are perhaps influenced by the same idea. Police were never able to identify nor find all the victims' bodies. This story of Dr. H. H. Holmes is a terrifying tale of gruesome proportions that may remind us of these evils that truly exist.

9

DEMON HOUSE, THE GATEWAY TO HELL

In a small town in Indiana, a woman claimed demons possessed her and her three children. The police department declared the case to be the most bizarre story they had ever witnessed. A family case manager and hospital nurse saw one of the children walking backward up a wall. At first, many believed it to be a hoax that the family concocted to earn money from the strange story. However, after 800 pages of investigations that detailed the demonic occurrences, even the police officers were claiming they believed the family was possessed.

The events started in November 2011, when Latoya Ammons' family moved into their new rental house in a quiet suburban area of Gary, Indiana. Suddenly, in December, giant black flies swarmed the screened porch of their home, despite the freezing temperatures and the snow. Most nights at midnight, Latoya Ammons heard loud footsteps marching up the basement stairs and the sound of the door opening from the basement to the kitchen even though no one was there. Latoya tried locking the door, but the sounds continued.

One night, when Latoya had fallen asleep on the living room sofa, she awoke to a broad dark figure pacing in her living room. When she turned on the light, however, the figure was gone, but big wet boot prints were left behind. Three months later, the initial spookiness of the house took a frightening turn towards real fear.

One night, at around 2 AM, while the family gathered in the Ammons' house to mourn the death of a close family friend, Latoya suddenly heard one of her children yelling, "Mama, Mama!" She arrived at the bedroom that her daughter slept in and found her body levitating above the bed, and her daughter completely unconscious. Family members gathered around the bed and began to pray. Eventually, her body descended back onto the bed, and her daughter awoke without any memory of the event.

Latoya was terrified and realized that she was dealing with someone or something that was outside of her experience. She started calling several churches in the area, many of whom refused to even listen to her. Finally, one church did respond, stating that they were aware of the spirits that lived on Carolina Street. The officials at the church told Latoya to cleanse the house top to bottom with bleach and ammonia. Then take oil and make crosses on every one of the doors and windows in the house, pour oil on her children's hands and feet, and make a cross shape with the oil on their foreheads.

Latoya's mother, Rosa Campbell, was living with the Ammons' during this time and was significant support for the family during this difficult time. They consulted two clairvoyants who stated that over 200 demons were occupying the house, something Latoya was quick to believe because of her deep Christian faith. The psychics told the family that they needed to move out immediately to be safe from the spirits that resided in the home. However, Latoya and her family had just moved there and now could not afford to relocate.

The next piece of advice that the clairvoyant gave Latoya since she could not afford to move out of the house was to make an altar in the basement. Using an end table covered with a white sheet as the altar, a white candle placed on the table with a statue of Jesus, Mary, and Joseph as a symbol of faith. Then read Psalm 91 from the Bible while standing at the altar.

Reading The Psalm aloud:

"You will not fear the terror of the night,

nor the arrow that flies by day,

nor the pestilence that talks in the darkness,

nor the plague that destroys at midday."

- Psalm 91

The attendants at the reading all wore white t-shirts and wrapped white pieces of fabric around their heads. The smoke produced from sage and sulfur wound around the hallways and rooms of the house; the smoke was so thick throughout the whole house; many of the guests had trouble breathing.

After the meeting and prayers by the altar in the basement, nothing odd happened in the house for three days. Then, after the third day, things got much worse. Demons started possessing the children and Latoya's bodies.

Latoya claimed to have been born with a special kind of protection from demons. Thus the demons were unable to possess her body successfully. However, her children were vulnerable and would break out in evil smiles, suddenly have deep voices, and their eyes would bulge.

Her seven-year-old son, who was once violently thrown out of the bathroom. Hitting his head on a headboard and requiring stitches, was found talking to an invisible boy in his closet. The ghostly child was describing to him what it was like to die. The oldest daughter told mental health professionals that at times she would feel like she was being choked and held down, unable to move or speak. A voice whispered into her ear, saying she would never see her family again and wouldn't live another 20 minutes.

Latoya finally took the children to the doctor to discuss what she could do to fix this. Dr. Geoffrey Onyeokwu described the visit as the most bizarre meeting he had ever had in his entire career. He even claimed to be frightened when he walked into the room. Suddenly, the seven-year-old boy began cursing the doctor in demonic voices. Witnesses said that the young boy was then suddenly thrown into a wall with no one touching him.

An unidentified witness called the Department of Child Services and instructed them to investigate Latoya, claiming that she had a mental illness and that her children were performing for her and encouraging her illness. However, after examining Latoya and her children, they were determined healthy, free of any bruises, scars, or marks. Latoya was deemed "of a sound mind."

Hospital staff interviewed the children once more. During the interview, the youngest son suddenly began growling at his older brother and said: "I'm going to kill you." The youngest child then walked back up the wall to the ceiling and flipped over his older brother. Both examiners ran from the room at the sight of this.

These strange episodes continued to occur through the year 2012 and into 2013. People would visit the house and suddenly become deathly ill for over a week; Latoya broke three ribs, broke her hand, and then broke her ankle, all within a matter of a few months. Unexplained smells and sounds emanated from the house.

The family participated in three exorcisms.

These exorcisms were the first to be sanctioned, unofficially, by the Catholic Church in Gary, Indiana. The first exorcism was comprised of a "minor ritual" and was similarly performed like the previous session in the basement using the white altar. After this "minor ritual," Latoya was told that she needed to write down the names of all the demons; each demon had a name and a specific personality. The names possessed power, and the priest was to use this power to condemn the demons.

During this exorcism, her body convulsed violently, and Latoya could feel both a sense of pain in her body while at the same time, something fighting to stay with her.

The priest stated the demons were strong, based on how

Latoya's body was convulsing. Two police officers stood by guarding and watching the event. The Ammon's prayed with their priest until they could no longer stand. Latoya began to hurt "from the inside out" and eventually passed out.

In the final exorcism, the leader berated the demons in Latin, as the previous two were in English, commanding them to leave.

Latoya convulsed while condemning the demons. After this last exorcism, the family was able to live in peace finally.

For six months, Latoya's children were taken from her by child services. However, soon after the last exorcism, her children were returned to her. They live in Indianapolis now, far from the house on Carolina Street that they once called home.

The landlord of the house claimed that he never had any issues at home before the Ammons' and after they moved out. He was as perplexed as to the medical examiners, hospital staff, and police officers. No one was able to ever explain the seeming paranormal occurrences outside of claiming that demonic forces had indeed possessed the Ammons family.

The Ammons family's story is just one of many demonic possession cases throughout history, with exorcisms dating back hundreds of thousands of years. The Catholic Church used to perform exorcisms regularly. However, they have become rarer in the last century. There is no doubt this family suffered inexplicably for months and experienced great, unnatural fear. They are now thankful to be free at last.

Zak Bagans, the host of the tv show "Ghost Adventures," purchased the house in 2016. He demolished the house soon after, stating, "Something was inside that house that could do things that he'd never seen before. There was something very dark yet highly intelligent and powerful there."

THE AGONY OF ANNELIESE MICHEL

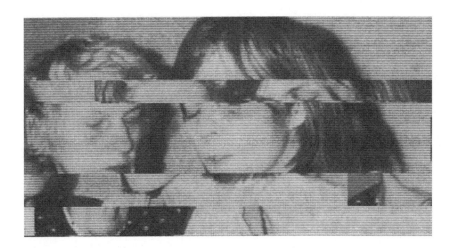

I f you happen to be a fan of horror novels, and especially movies, it's possible that you already know of a film called "The Exorcism of Emily Rose." What you might not know, however, is that this movie was based loosely on the terrible story of Anneliese Michel.

Anneliese was a German girl who lived in Bavaria and was born in 1952 to a devout Catholic family. She was off to a relatively routine start as a young girl, and it's unlikely that anyone could have predicted the tragic fate that would befall her in her teen years. She was sixteen when she suffered her first seizure, and doctors diagnosed her with epilepsy. Not long after that, Anneliese began to suffer from extreme depression that landed her in a psychiatric hospital in 1973.

Much more peculiar than her apparent mental problems were the other symptoms that followed. Anneliese would hear voices that appeared to damn her to hell. She would experience nightmarish hallucinations, particularly when praying. Anneliese was describing these as demonic messages from the Devil himself. She also started developing a strong aversion towards any religious items and began to perceive strange sounds, such as knocking in her room. These sounds were reported by her sisters, too.

What seemed to be merely a mental health issue quickly started to adopt a much more sinister property. The prescribed medication didn't seem to help the poor girl either, and according to some sources, her brain scans would repeatedly come back contrary.

At that point, Anneliese herself started to believe multiple evil presences possessed her. As her condition worsened, she also began seeing demonic faces, both on people and objects that surrounded her. Things got so bad at one point that

Anneliese would deprive herself of sleep and a regular diet. She even ate bugs and started to consume her urine.

Anneliese spoke of these haunting experiences to her doctor and voiced her belief that she was possessed. Doctors couldn't be of much help in this regard, though, so Anneliese and her family soon abandoned their search for help through medical means. In 1975, the Catholic clergy decided Anneliese needed the help to rid her of the demons.

The church was hesitant to get involved at first, and priests needed the permission of their archbishop to perform an exorcism. A priest by the name of Ernst Alt was interested in the case and believed what was happening to Anneliese was real. But his requests to perform the ritual were denied. Finally, in September of 1975, Bishop Josef Stangl decided to allow Arnold Renz to exorcise Anneliese Michel.

The Bishop gave Renz the go-ahead to use a four-hundred-year-old exorcism ritual called Rituale Romanum, but he was to conduct it himself in secrecy. The use of this old ritual garnered much public attention later on. Father Renz performed the first ritual on September 24, and Alt also participated then on. Anneliese was entirely on board with the exorcisms and voluntarily fought the perceived demons inside her. The exorcisms went on for around ten months from that point on, totaling sixty-seven rituals at the end.

Renz also permitted to record a number of these rituals, and the chilling audio recordings exist to this day, available for anyone to hear online. The exorcisms themselves were excruciating, with Anneliese convulsing and exhibiting a lot of the usual demonic behaviors associated with such incidents. Mainly striking was one instance where she spoke of the demons inside of her, naming Lucifer, Judas, Cain, and even Hitler as her tormentors. However, the most shocking was her mention of a priest called Fleischmann. The church banished him from his service before the exorcism. He was someone Anneliese should not have had any knowledge of, yet she did.

As the exorcisms were underway, things got progressively darker for Anneliese. Soon enough, Anneliese started to forgo nutrition and even water, which was made even more dangerous by the fact that the family had already stopped seeking any kind of medical assistance for Anneliese. She felt that fasting would weaken the hold that this perceived evil force had on her, so it was voluntary.

Furthermore, Anneliese was obsessed with performing genuflections, the act of bending a knee, aiming to do hundreds of them during each ritual. After a while, this took a severe toll and left her with acute knee injuries. The malnutrition left her body a frail mess, with her weight dropping below seventy pounds. Towards the end, Anneliese was too weak to move on her own, and it's believed that she got pneumonia. After a while, Anneliese became increasingly engulfed with ideas of dying to atone for the sins of others. Mainly of the youth and the apostates of the Catholic

Church. And die she did, on July 1st of 1976, when she finally succumbed to her terrible state at the age of 23. She weighed only sixty-eight pounds when she died, reduced to but a shell of her former, healthy self. Declaring Her death as being caused by malnutrition and dehydration, and her pneumonia and fever only sped up the process.

It's also said by some sources that Anneliese spoke foreign languages through her outbursts during the exorcisms. With some of those instances possibly being recorded on the existing tapes. Her voice undoubtedly disfigured and unrecognizable, much following other cases of possession.

What exactly happened to Anneliese Michel was an object of a heated debate for years and remained contested to this day. Her parents, together with the two priests who performed the exorcisms, were charged and convicted of negligent homicide for failing to provide Anneliese with the necessary nutrition, water, and medical assistance. They were released immediately on probation, but the sentences stuck.

Significantly working toward the arguments that Anneliese was simply a deeply troubled young lady who didn't receive the proper attention that she needed, but a few things speak to the counterpoint, also. The light sentence is undoubtedly a testament to the fact that quite a few folks saw the whole thing as a demon at work. The horrifying recordings, of which there were more than forty, obviously compelled the court to some extent. These recordings are readily available to everyone, but be warned that they are deeply unsettling.

The fact is, though, whether Anneliese was indeed possessed or just mentally ill, she was not in a position to reason and make healthy decisions for herself, the proof of which was her refusal to eat, ultimately leading her to death. This fact means that the veracity of the possession claim wasn't on trial. It was the responsibility of the priests, and the parents put on the stand. And indeed, whatever it was that occurred to poor Anneliese, it's undeniable that more could have been done to prevent her death.

Many folks have subsequently gone on to denote the case of Anneliese Michel as a textbook example of misinterpretation of mental illness and outright religious fanaticism. Others still believe she was indeed possessed, which is what the parents thought in the years that followed.

With all the suffering she endured, Anneliese was disturbed once again in 1978. Two years after her funeral, exhuming her body due to the parents' wishes. Giving her a better coffin and relocating her remains within the cemetery. It's also worth mentioning that the Church later issued an official statement saying that they consider this to have been a case of mental illness, not a possession.

Whatever form of evil it was that afflicted Anneliese, whether it was earthly or demonic, her short life was indeed one of immense agony and horror.

SELF-CONFESSED CANNIBAL

I n the natural world of survival, the sight of a predatory animal eating its prey can be gruesome. Also, in the animal world, there are specific examples of a cannibal species, such as the Black Widow spider and the Praying Mantis, which eat their kind. What could be more shocking?

Well, what about a human eating another human? And what if such human cannibalism is not so much about natural survival instincts, but instead because of pre-meditated, disturbed, and psychological murderous intention?

This story is about Yoo Young-Chul, a South Korean, who claimed to have killed 21 people in about ten months. Most of his victims were either elderly, rich people, or prostitutes. While multiple murders are shocking in itself, this is not what made Yoo famous - or notorious - for. It is the fact that he confessed to not only killing but also ingesting the body parts of his victims. So prolific (twenty-one murders in ten months!) and horrific were his crimes, including him to a list of the worst serial killers in the world.

Born in 1970, Yoo was the child of working-class parents who separated soon after he was born. Yoo, along with his siblings, was sent to stay with their grandmother. She took care of them for a few years, and then the children went to their father, who lived in Seoul. His parents weren't flush with money, a fact that made him the target of a lot of taunts at school. As a result of this bullying, Yoo started feeling resentful towards the wealthy upper-class members of society.

The school was also where Yoo discovered his passion for the arts. In elementary school, he wrote poetry, played the guitar, painted and sang. His interest in these fields was such that Yoo tried to get admission to a high school that specialized in these subjects. Rejecting his application, he settled for a technical school.

It was in high school that Yoo began his life of crime. He started by stealing, probably as a means of providing for his impoverished family. He was caught and sent to juvenile detention. This incarceration did not deter him, and as soon as he was out, he continued his career in thievery. He stole cash, electronics, and even cars. He spent a lot of time in jail during the 90s due to his propensity for theft.

He got married sometime in 1992 and had one son. Things turned bad for Yoo once more in the year 2000 when police arrested him for the rape of a 15-year-old girl. While he was serving out his prison sentence, his wife served him with divorce papers.

After his release in 2002, Yoo descended into a complete criminal life. He made his living by extorting money from prostitutes and pimps by posing as a policeman complete with a fake ID. When this didn't seem lucrative enough, he graduated to murder.

On September 1, 2003, Yoo broke into the home of an elderly couple in the wealthy district of Gangnam-gu in Seoul. He stabbed the husband in the neck and then bashed his head in with a hammer. Yoo then moved on to the wife, who he also killed with the same hammer. He made the crime look like a robbery-murder but didn't take any cash from the house, thereby puzzling the authorities.

About a month later, he again invaded a home in Jongro-gu. This time, there were three occupants aged eighty-five, sixty, and thirty-five. Yoo used his trademark hammer again to murder all three people. The next day he got into the house of an older woman, who he brutally attacked with the hammer and then left her for dead. Her son found her with gruesome injuries and called for medical assistance, but he was too late. She died half an hour later.

In November, he broke into another house. This time, he did things differently from his previous modus operandi. After killing the two occupants, he tried to open a safe but was injured. Afraid that DNA evidence would identify him, Yoo burned down the house. There was a baby in the house at the time it was set on fire. And the infant, unfortunately, perished.

In December, Yoo met and fell in love with a woman who was a prostitute. However, when she found out about his criminal past, she told him that she wanted nothing to do with him. This bluntness enraged Yoo and set him on a different path. He decided to focus his anger on killing prostitutes.

From March to July 2004, Yoo killed eleven prostitutes. The first murder was slightly different from the rest. Yoo posed as a potential customer and lured a prostitute away from her safety zone and area. He then strangled her, mutilated her corpse and left it lying in the trash of a construction site near Bongwon Temple.

For the rest of the murders, Yoo followed the same procedure. He would call masseuses over to his home, have sex with them, and murder them with the hammer. Yoo would then mutilate or dismember their bodies, so they weren't easily identified. He took the bodies into the forests around Seoul and disposed of them.

The murders alarmed not only the police and the general public but also pimps, to the point they cooperated with police in the hunt for the killer. On 15 July 2004, Yoo made a call to a massage parlor asking the parlor to send a masseuse over. Several masseuses had gone missing previously, and for each one, the call had come from the same number. The owner of the parlor realized this and contacted the police. Accompanied by one police officer and several employees, the owner then went to the agreed-upon meeting place. Because he got to the appointed place late, Yoo initially avoided capture since the police officer had already left.

However, when Yoo arrived, the owner and employees promptly surrounded him, a police officer handcuffed and arrested Yoo. However, while in custody, Yoo managed to escape by faking an epileptic fit, something he had done successfully earlier after being arrested on charges of rape. His freedom didn't last long, though, and he was apprehended twelve hours later.

Initially, after his arrest, Yoo confessed to nineteen murders. He said that he had targeted wealthy people and masseuses. When police searched his apartment, they found material that led them to believe that he had patterned his murders on several movies, including "Normal Life" and "Public Enemy." Yoo himself professed that his inspiration was another South Korean serial killer, Jeong Du-Yeong, who also targeted the wealthy.

Yoo said that he went after rich people because of the humiliation he had suffered in school as a child and the resentment he bore them as a result. The masseuses he murdered were his way of taking revenge on his lover. Who ended their relationship after finding out about his criminal past. Yoo even confessing to thoughts of killing his ex-wife But decided against it for the sake of his son.

Sometime after his arrest, Yoo revealed that he had committed additional murders not included in the ones publicized, starting with a male street vendor. Friends of two of the masseuses that Yoo had murdered came forward, stating that these women hadn't been prostitutes. This confession raised suspicions that Yoo wasn't just targeting two types of victims. Many days later, he said that he had killed a young woman who worked in a clothing store, but due to technicalities, this case wasn't included in his list of convictions. Chillingly, Yoo said that he had consumed the livers of some of his victims.

His trial was bizarre. The police did not have much physical evidence to connect Yoo to the crimes. It was his confessions that brought him down. He first refused to defend himself, saying that he would boycott the remainder of the trial and even apologized to the victims. Later, he boasted that if he were released, he would not stop committing such murders. Two weeks later, at his hearing, he took back the confession about the girl in the clothing store and also lunged at the judges. He tried to kill himself on the night before the next trial date and disrupted another trial three weeks later. The judge forced him into signing a statement saying that he wouldn't cause any more disruptions.

The prosecution asked for the death penalty, for which Yoo expressed his gratitude. He was sentenced to death on December 13, 2004, on twenty counts of murder.

The court, when handing out its verdict, said, "Murders of as many as 20 people are unprecedented in the nation and a severe crime. The death penalty is inevitable for you in light of the enormous pains inflicted on the families concerned and the entire society."

Yoo's crime spree had served to increase the debate raging throughout South Korea on the necessity of the death penalty. Public opinion - which before the trial, had swerved towards the abolition of the death penalty - is now increasingly in support of it, considering the horrific nature of Yoo's crimes.

1 2

MISSING BOY

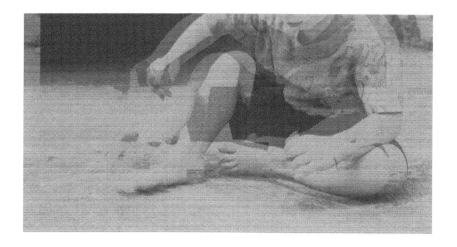

The disappearance of Timmothy Pitzen and his mother's (Amy Pitzen) suicide made headlines when it happened in 2011. The case became notorious, not only because of the strange circumstances surrounding it but also because of the mystery surrounding the boy's whereabouts.

Until this day, no one is aware of the actual causes that led to the events on May 11, 2011, and where Timmothy Pitzen is now. The mysterious and sad fact has prompted a lot of speculation and theories about what happened and why.

Timmothy Pitzen is the son of James and Amy Joan Marie Fry-Pitzen. The family lived in Aurora, Illinois, and Timmothy was six-years-old at the time of his disappearance. On May 11, 2011, Amy went to Timmothy's school, the Greenman Elementary School, and removed him from his kindergarten class. She did not inform James or any of the relatives of her plans. After she took him from the school, she took her car, a blue 2004 Ford Expedition SUV, to an auto repair shop and dropped it off. The time was ten in the morning. She asked one of the repair shop employees to drive her and Timmothy to the Brookfield Zoo, which he did. After spending time at the zoo, she came back to the auto repair shop at 3 p.m. They fixed her vehicle. She then took Timmothy to the KeyLime Cove Resort, located in Gurnee, Illinois. They spent the night there.

In the meantime, Timothy's father, James, arrived at the school to pick him up. When he found out that Amy had already checked Timmothy out earlier in the day, he tried calling Amy on her cellphone many times but couldn't reach her. He eventually filed a missing person's report for them.

The next day Amy took Timmothy to Wisconsin Dells, Wisconsin, and checked into the Kalahari Resort. The next day she and Timmothy were seen on the security camera footage waiting to check out at ten o'clock in the morning. At half-past one in the afternoon, Amy called several of her family members and told them that she and Timmothy were safe and alright. The family members could hear Timmothy in the background. He sounded fine and, at one point, even mentioned that he was hungry. Oblivious to the family, this was the last time he was heard from again.

On the evening of the same day, at twenty-five minutes past seven, people saw Amy in Winnebago, Illinois, at a Family Dollar store. There was no sign of Timmothy. She bought some stationary and then went to Sullivan's Foods nearby at eight o'clock. Between 11:30 and 11:45, she checked into the Rockford Inn in Rockford, Illinois. Timmothy wasn't with her here, either. That night, Amy Pitzen took an overdose of antihistamines and then slashed her wrists and her throat. At the time that she took her life, Amy was forty-three years old. At half-past-twelve in the afternoon, her corpse was found by the Inn's employees on May 14.

Sometime later, a suicide letter from Amy made its way to her mother. In the letter, Amy said that she felt that she didn't fit in with everyone, even though she had tried hard to do so. She implied that her relationship with her husband James wasn't good anymore and said that she couldn't pick up the pieces.

After this, the note became cryptic. Amy said that she couldn't take the risk that James would hurt Timmothy because of the choices she made. She took Timmothy somewhere safe where he would be 'well cared for.' She then apologized for the hurt and difficulties that her family would have to face and asked for forgiveness. In another note sent to a friend, Amy said that no one would ever find Timmothy.

When investigators started looking into the disappearance of the boy and Amy's suicide, it came to light that her cellphone was missing. That wasn't the only item. Timmothy's toys, clothes, his Spiderman backpack, the clothes that Amy had been wearing at the Kalahari Resort, an iPass transponder, and a Crest toothpaste tube had also disappeared.

At first, authorities believed that Amy had indeed left Timmothy with people who would care for him. This belief seemed to be backed up by the fact that they couldn't find the little boy's car seat. However, it later turned out that the car seat was with Timmothy's grandmother, who lived in Wooster, Ohio. It had been with her for a week before the disappearance. This information and the fact that several days already passed without any sign of the boy got the police and the family extremely worried.

Sometime later, the police made a disturbing discovery. There were traces of blood in the backseat of Amy's SUV. Upon analysis, it turned out that the blood was Timmothy's, although it was impossible to tell how long the blood had been in the vehicle. Further investigations revealed that the boy's relatives said that about twelve to eighteen months before his disappearance, he had suffered from a bloody nose inside the vehicle. When examining the knife, Amy used to kill herself; the only blood on it was her own.

New forensic evidence came up when finding Amy's SUV. The vehicle was 'visibly dirty' as per the reports. Weeds, tall grass, and soil stuck to the undercarriage. The forensic test indicated that at some point, the car stopped in a graveled area for a while. This graveled area was very close to an asphalt road treated with glass road-making beads at some point in time. It seemed that Amy backed the vehicle into a grassy field. Evidence indicated that this field probably did not have any trees and contained black mustard plants and Queen Anne's lace. Investigators speculated that there could be some birch or oak trees in that area, although not in the clearing where the car was. Investigators also believed that there would be a small pond or stream nearby. All this evidence, however, couldn't help the investigators narrow down the possibilities to just one.

Upon further inquiries, it came to light that Amy had been behaving strangely and may have planned her son's disap-pearance for some time. She made two trips in February and March 2011 to the area from which Timmothy eventually disappeared. She also created an email account registered to her maiden name and which her husband James didn't know about; however, no emails related to the disappearance were on the account. Investigators discovered that Amy was clini-cally depressed and often left her home for long periods.

Amy's husband and relatives were mystified and heartbroken

by these events. James said that he couldn't believe that Amy would do anything to hurt Timmothy. Both he and her relatives agreed that she loved her son a lot. None of the family members suspected him whisked away. No further evidence was forthcoming.

Sometime in 2013, Amy's cellphone was discovered lying on the side of the road on Route 78. Immediately, the investigators went to search the area for more clues but didn't find anything else. The cellphone turned out to be a dead-end too.

These facts are all we know to this day. There is no sign of Timmothy and no clue as to his whereabouts. That hasn't stopped netizens from speculating about what could have happened. There have been various theories put forward, most of them centering on Amy's note to her mother.

People have wondered why Amy would believe that Timmothy would suffer his father's retaliation for her actions. Some point out that Amy was known to suffer from depression and may have exaggerated her fears. Others speculate that James wasn't Timmothy's birth father, and Amy was afraid of how he would treat Timmothy if he found out.

The most chilling aspect of the letter Amy wrote is that she categorically stated no one would ever find the little boy, also, saying Timmothy would be well taken care of. People feel she may have left her son with somebody who she trusted and would protect Timmothy from the uproar surrounding his disappearance. Others are not so optimistic. They believe she knew she couldn't trust anyone to take on the consequences of hiding Timmothy. Since she was planning to take her own life, she may have killed Timmothy as well. The phrase 'well cared for' could be interpreted to mean that he is in Heaven.

There have also been rumors of Amy involved in a cult of some sort. What this cult was, whether it had anything to do with Timmothy's disappearance and whether she was, in fact, part of any cult at all, is pure speculation. Whatever the theories presented, one thing is sure. From May 13, 2011, until now, nobody has laid eyes on Timmothy Pitzen.

13

THE VANISHING YOUTUBERS

Youtubers are certainly an interesting phenomenon of our time in their own right, with their ability to amass vast numbers of followers who will tune in regularly to consume the content that they produce. Therefore, when it concerns large channels, every disappearance, no matter how short, usually stirs up a lot of controversies and leaves a lot of people guessing as to what might be going on.

When it's a famous person, mysteries resolve pretty quickly, as was the case with a channel called FPS Russia, for instance. This large channel is hosted by Kyle Myers from the US, boasting over six million subscribers. Kyle assumes the role of a Russian man with a thick Eastern European accent, who showcases and demonstrates the effects of many different types of weaponry and explosives.

A wave of controversy resonated throughout YouTube after Kyle mysteriously vanished from the platform in the spring of 2013. Without any announcement or foreshadowing whatsoever, the channel simply stopped uploading. The assumptions of what happened ranged from the man being dead or having become tired of YouTube, all the way to him merely taking a vacation. Some nine months later, Kyle reappeared with a new video, and some answers began cropping up.

Namely, it turned out that a crucial member of the channel's crew, Keith Ratliff, who was in charge of acquiring the weapons for Kyle's videos, was found shot in the back of his head early in 2013, seemingly execution-style. Federal agents stormed that spring, Kyle's house in Georgia from the ATF and FBI. Kyle's father's farm, a location for many of the channel's videos, was also searched by the agents. The authorities gave conflicting statements as to the cause for these searches, with ATF stating that they were looking into possibly illegal explosives in Kyle's possession. Interestingly enough, the country sheriff said that the searches were in connection with the murder of Kyle's colleague, which effectively meant that FPS Russia himself was a suspect.

Keith's murder remains unsolved, with minimal information released by the police. This mystery made the crime one of the most peculiar of the YouTube community and, of course, an object of many conspiracy theories and speculations. Whatever the case may have been, no charges were brought forward against Kyle. He has since been active on and off with his channel, without much mention of these events.

As always, the case with large channels, as someone among the millions of fans, are bound to dig something up sooner or later. For this reason, smaller channels are far more unusual and unsettling. One such example is the story of Kenny Veach, who vanished in the deserts of Nevada on November 10, 2014. Kenny was an enthusiast for the outdoors and had an apparent liking for thrills and dares, as long-distance hiking was a passion of his. He also liked to challenge snakes and otherwise tackle nature as a hobby, garnering considerable hiking experience as a result. He was by no means a dedicated Youtuber, but his channel, called "snakebitmgee," was where this story began around a month before his disappearance. Namely, Kenny left a comment on a video titled "Son of an Area 51 Technician," telling in a few sentences his personal story from the desert.

He claimed he was hiking in the proximity of the Nellis Air

Force Base in the Nevada desert when he stumbled upon a peculiar cave somewhere in the Sheep Mountains. He described the cave as being secluded and having an entrance shaped like a perfect, capital letter "M." In his usual fashion, he wanted to enter and explore the cave, but as he began to approach the strange entrance, he felt his body starting to vibrate. Kenny said that the vibrations grew more intense the closer he got to the opening. Suddenly, he was overcome by dread and decided to run away, as this feeling was unlike anything he encountered before.

Kenny's comment sparked a lengthy thread of replies from those who were captivated by the account, and many demanded proof. Motivated to oblige, Kenny decided to take another ten-hour hike back to the location and record footage of the cave for his channel. He later uploaded footage of his trip, although he was unable to relocate the M cave. As a significant number of folks were teeming with interest at this point, Kenny vowed to take a third trip and acquire his evidence.

Online, he stated that this new trip would be better organized and that he would bring his pistol with him this time. He went on to explain that it's a ten-hour hike over very rough, dangerous terrain. Some people challenged him, but others implored him not to go back. Particularly strange comment on his video urged him not to go back to the cave, saying that if he found the cave entrance and went in, he wouldn't come out. Kenny responded, asking why the poster would say this, but he never got a response. Despite everything, finding the cave seemed to have become a matter of pride and challenge for Kenny, and he was unrelenting in his desire to see the mysterious cave.

He ventured back out into the wilderness on November 10th, never to return. His family quickly became concerned, informing authorities of his disappearance. Search and rescue efforts performed with no result, but the only sign of the explorer was his cell phone, dropped next to a deep, vertical mineshaft. Of course, it looked as if he plunged to his death. But a search of the mine didn't turn up a single shred of evidence of his presence. No trails were found in the vicinity either, and a more extensive search returned no further results. Kenny had simply vanished.

Speculations ran wild soon after that. Some assumed that Kenny simply lost his way and died of exposure to the brutal desert or its wildlife. Others purported that he encountered smugglers that killed him. Seeing as the whole ordeal began with a comment on a documentary video concerning aliens and government cover-ups, there was no shortage of paranormal and government foul play explanations either. Anything from alien abduction to government liquidation was a possibility.

A feasible explanation some ascribed to was that Kenny either faked his death or committed suicide. This thought is perhaps corroborated by the later-learned information that

Kenny was going through some hard times financially and acquiring debt.

Things got even more contrived when his girlfriend posted a lengthy comment on his M cave search video, stating that she believes that Kenny had indeed committed suicide. She mentioned that Kenny experienced depression in the past and discussed suicide with her on a couple of occasions. Most peculiarly, she said that Kenny hypothesized that if he ever decided to do it, nobody would ever be able to find him.

While the story of his communications on social media and his disappearance is one that's easily confirmable, no conclusive results have ever come about from any investigation. Did Kenny stumble upon something that he shouldn't have seen, or was the whole story just an elaborate ploy to commit the perfect suicide or vanish into a new life? Anything is possible when details are so scarce, but everything that led up to Kenny Veach's disappearance has a certain eerie, dreadful legitimacy to it.

14

THE DARK SIDE OF YOUTUBE

For most people, YouTube is but a place for quick, harmless, innocent entertainment, which usually involves cute pets, funny videos of people falling off trampolines, or children acting foolishly. However, as you have gathered from the previous chapter or perhaps through your web surfing, all kinds of other things can be found on the platform as well.

Sometimes, one can run into some deeply unsettling content, even from those channels that don't specifically deal with shocking people or producing scary content. Still, it just turns out that way sometimes. In that regard, some Youtubers have encountered a range of disturbing sights while creating their content over the years, with some of them ending up with dead bodies on their cameras – knowingly or not.

One video of this kind was uploaded by a user who goes by the name of "marcelstjean" in 2014. He is a Canadian vlogger with a modest following of a little over eleven-thousand subscribers on YouTube as of right now. On that particular day, marcelstjean was shooting footage on his way to a festival in Ontario, when he crossed paths in the street with a group of men who were visibly drunk or otherwise intoxicated.

Three of the men were talking and drunkenly stumbling around the place. The Two others were lying on the pavement near a building, with a nearly empty bottle next to them. The vlogger decided to get closer and check on them to see if they were okay, believing they were just drunk out of their minds.

He inspected the first man whose face was covered by a hoodie only to discover that he was indeed just passed out drunk. However, as soon as the man started to inspect the other person, it became apparent that he was eerily cold and unresponsive. He checked the poor man's pulse, and it quickly became clear that the individual was most likely dead.

Despite the sudden realization that they were filming a dead man, marcelstjean and his companion remained calm and composed. They immediately called an ambulance, which showed up promptly and sorted out the situation. The police also arrived to question witnesses, and the tragic ordeal thus came to its conclusion.

Abandoned buildings

Apart from good old-fashioned vlogging, another trend that has gained significant momentum in recent years is urban exploration, which has a considerable base right on YouTube. These folks make an interesting hobby out of exploring old, abandoned buildings, such as factories, hospitals, prisons, apartment complexes, or even funeral homes.

An old funeral home called Memorial Mound was what a group of explorers led by Matt Glasscock explored in 2015, in the proximity of Birmingham, Alabama. Initially, they found just what you would expect of an abandoned funeral home: a lot of dust, quite a few coffins, and a bone-chilling atmosphere.

However, when they started to inspect the premises further and opened a few of the coffins, for whatever reason, they found that one of them contained what appeared to be a duffel bag full of human remains. These were mostly bones, and the team of explorers captured and uploaded footage showing the remains of at least one long-decomposed corpse. You can still see this video on Matt's YouTube channel.

Not long after his discovery, the police got involved, and they ultimately identified remains of eight people left behind at the mausoleum, one of whom was an infant. How exactly the remains of eight bodies managed to slip through the cracks, so to speak, and be left lying around an abandoned funeral home remains an object of some mystery. The police and the local coroner's office promptly initiated the process of getting in touch with the families and relatives of the deceased to make final arrangements.

Blood-soaked sheets

There are many other instances of urban explorers supposedly running into corpses on their adventures, but a lot of the incidents are likely faked. One particularly disturbing and convincing video was uploaded in 2016 by a relatively large channel belonging to Uosof Ahmadi. The video shows him and a friend trying to get into an abandoned house at night. Unable to get through the door, the two climbed up to take a look inside through one of the bare window openings, only to find and record what appears to be a body wrapped up in blood-soaked white sheets.

The two then promptly run away, and the video cuts to footage of an ambulance nearby. While certainly unsettling and convincing, the video's veracity is greatly diminished by a lack of official stories and articles on the incident, as well as by the fact that the channel has a range of other, similar videos. Be that as it may, the video is certainly worth taking a look at, as it is most definitely a piece of quality horror and macabre.

While it's sometimes difficult to tell what is real and what is a mere publicity stunt, it's certainly not hard to imagine that people who explore such areas in major urban centers are undoubtedly likely to run into something unpleasant sooner or later. This reality holds especially true for places with a considerable rate of violent crime, and it would be less than surprising to see an urban explorer get more than he bargained for, one of these days.

15

RUNNING FOR YOUR LIFE

There has been a lot of conjecture about the disappearance of Lars Mittank. Netizens around the world have wondered what caused Mittank to behave so bizarrely and then disappear the way he did. All sorts of theories have been imagined– from erratic behavior due to injury to the brain to genuine fear that someone was out to get him. One thing is for sure. In 2014, Mittank was caught on surveillance cameras behaving very strangely, and shortly afterward, he vanished. No one to this day knows what happened to the young man.

In July 2014, Lars Mittank, a 28-year-old German tourist, went on a vacation to Bulgaria with a couple of his friends. The Golden Sands in Bulgaria, where Mittank and his friends headed, is a popular destination for the young tourist crowd from Germany and England. During this vacation, he was partying on the beach one day when he got into a fight with some other tourists. It appears that the two parties were fighting about football. Mittank was an ardent fan of the Werder Bremen football club. He got in the face of some Bulgarian or Russian supporters of the Bayern Munich team. As seems only natural where football is concerned, the argument turned into an all-out brawl.

Mittank suffered a minor injury in his ear as a result of the fight. When his vacation drew to a close, he approached a doctor about the wound. The doctor told him not to fly and gave him an antibiotic known as Cefuroxime 500. He also advised Mittank to go to a hospital.

It seems that Mittank decided to take the doctor's advice and stay on in Bulgaria for further treatment. He told his friends to return to Germany without him and rented a room in a hostel located in the seedier section of town. It was the last time they saw him.

That night he called his mother and told her that he feared for his life. He begged her to have his credit card canceled and said to her that he was afraid someone was following him. He said that he "...was being followed by four men..." and they had asked him what the pills he was carrying were for (they were the antibiotics the doctor had prescribed).

The next day Mittank headed to the airport. What happened next is captured on the surveillance cameras inside and outside the airport. At first, you can see Mittank walking normally, if a bit quickly, into the airport pulling his luggage along. A surveillance camera shows him going into the doctor's office at the airport. So far, so good.

What comes next is the creepy part. After some time, you can see Mittank come running out of the doctor's office at top speed minus his bag and suitcase. A camera set up opposite the entrance and exit of the airport shows Mittank running erratically. The final footage, taken from an airport surveillance camera, shows Mittank running along the road in the distance. Suddenly he moves to his left and climbs over a fence. He runs into the forest that surrounds the airport. That is the last time anyone saw anything of him.

What caused Mittank to run out of the airport as though all the hounds from hell were after him. Some people think

Mittank's ear injury; he sustained due to the brawl, attributed to the erratic behavior. In the same vein, others believe that he suffered from a head injury because of the same fight, and that resulted in his paranoia and subsequent behavior.

However, there are darker theories out there. Some people believe that Mittank wasn't paranoid at all, nor was he afflicted with any traumatic injury that compromised his judgment. They think that the reasons for his fear were genuine. It could be the Russian or Bulgarian tourists he fought. The outcome of the fight isn't known, so it could be possible that they were stalking him to get even. When the police started investigating Mittank's disappearance, they asked for those tourists to come forward. No one did.

Another possibility is that Mittank saw or heard something at his hostel that he wasn't supposed to. The hostel, located in a part of town that is not so modern or upscale. He may have overheard a drug deal going down or something along those lines. His phone call to his mother certainly seems to indicate that he feared someone. He was specific enough to tell his mother to have his credit cards canceled. You could say that he didn't want anyone to be able to figure out where he was through his credit card purchases.

The way Mittank ran out of the doctor's office indicates he was purposeful. At first, you may think that he was chasing someone. But when you look carefully, you realize that he was running away from something or someone not towards it or him. Of course, what is entirely mind-boggling is the fact that he runs out of the airport and decides that the forest is his best hope for safety.

When the story of his disappearance aired in Bulgaria, a truck driver came forward and said that he had picked up someone who looked very much like Mittank, this happened around Easter of 2015. The person he picked up wanted to hitchhike and looked quite disheveled. There is no guarantee that this person was indeed Mittank.

Was Lars Mittank suffering from some sort of paranoia and delusion due to his ear injury or any head injury he may have received during the brawl? His decision to not fly back home because of the doctor's advice certainly seems to indicate the opposite. Moreover, the friends he was with did not specify that he had behaved erratically at all while he was with them after the injury.

So, does this mean that Mittank's fears were real? Was he terrified for his life? Who were the men he had brawled with on the beach? Why didn't they come forward when the police were making inquiries? Were they the same as the men Mittank believed were following him? If not, who were these new participants, and where did they come from? Why did they want to know what Lars' pills were for? What made Lars believe that his life was in danger at all? And finally, what made Lars Mittank run out of the doctor's office the way he did and disappear into the forest?

To this day, there are no specific answers to these questions. The airport surveillance camera footage has not explained much and only raise more conspiracy theories. The only person who knows what's going on is Mittank himself, and he is nowhere to be found.

DEMONS IN THE HOUSE

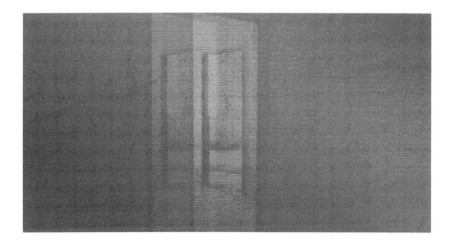

I magine that you finally found your dream home. It's a big house, a sprawling property, the right size to enter- tain visitors in gracefully, the perfect distance from work and school, and, most importantly, the right price. Ben and Jamie Shea found such a house. Hey, dreams can come true, right? But sometimes, we also forget that dreams can turn into nightmares too. What do they say about something that looks too good to be true? Let's find out.

In October 2003, Jamie and Ben Shea were looking for their dream home. They finally happened upon a house in Markham, Arkansas. The house was old but beautiful. It also had enough space to house their family of five: Jamie, Ben, and their three children, Tory, Bridger, and Jackson. There were beautiful trees around the house and plenty of room for the children to play. It was a short commute for Jamie, who worked as a legal assistant in a neighboring town and Ben, who worked as a nurse at a factory located nearby while earning his degree.

When the Sheas were viewing the house, they came across a bedroom on the second floor littered with candles, pentagrams, and other occult symbols. While the couple was initially disturbed by sight, they didn't overthink it. Ben assumed that local teenagers might have gotten into the house and just messed around. Without further ado, the couple made an offer on the house, and it was accepted.

The Shea family soon moved in and settled down to a routine. Ben worked the night shift at the factory and came home to sleep until two in the afternoon. He would then leave for his classes. Jamie hired an experienced babysitter to take care of Jackson, who was one year old. Everything seemed to be moving along fine.

One day, after Jamie had left for work, and the older two children were at school, Ben was fast asleep in their bedroom. The sitter was supposed to be taking care of little Jackson. Suddenly, Ben woke up with the sound of Jackson, their infant son, crying. The noise was coming from the baby monitor kept next to Ben's bed. At first, Ben thought nothing of it, calling out to the sitter to take care of the baby. The crying, however, persisted. Ben got up and called out to the sitter but got no answer. Groggily he made his way up the stairs to the baby's room, still calling the sitter. Ben again got no response. When he went inside the room, what he saw completely surprised him, Jackson wasn't in his crib. There was just the baby monitor.

Still no more than puzzled, Ben went back downstairs to the living room. There he found a note that the sitter had left saying that she'd taken the baby and gone shopping and would be back soon. There was no one in the house, apart from Ben. Baffled, he knew he hadn't imagined the cries. Yet there was no sign of where the noise could have come from, freaked out, he couldn't make heads or tails of what just happened. Ben decided to say nothing to Jamie about it.

Bridger, Ben, and Jamie's five-year-old son had the bedroom where they found the candles and symbols. Before he left for work, Ben made sure that he spent time tucking Bridger in. One night, after Ben had gone to work, Bridger was fast asleep when he was woken up in the middle of the night by loud noises. It sounded as though there were a lot of people in the room. They were all talking at once. Bridger was terrified. He ran out of his room and went to his parents' bedroom downstairs, where Jamie was sleeping. He told her that he had heard people talking in his bedroom. Jamie assumed that he was having nightmares and let him sleep with her.

On the same night, eight-year-old Tory, whose bedroom was down the hall from Bridger's, was woken up at around 3 a.m. by the sound of one of her brother's toys turning on. When she went to check out what was making the noise, she found out that the toys were lying all over the floor, and Bridger wasn't in his bed. Tory assumed that he was hiding, told him to put his toys away, and go back to sleep. But upon leaving the room, she heard the sound of many people talking at once. Frightened, she retreated to her bedroom.

The Shea didn't mention the strange happenings that they were witnessing to each other, and nothing else happened for a few more weeks. Then one night, while the kids were asleep and Jamie was sitting and working on some accounts, she suddenly heard footsteps. Jamie got up to investigate because it sounded as if the children were running up and down the staircase. She called out to them to get back into bed but got no response. When Jamie went back to the table where she had been working, there was a sudden bang in the next room, as if a door had just forcibly banged shut. When she ran back out, she saw no closed doors that could have made the banging sound. Jamie then went upstairs to check on her children and found them all fast asleep.

Soon after these incidents, the sitter told Jamie that she heard Jackson crying through the baby monitor. But when she went up to check on him, he was fast asleep. Jamie was disturbed enough that she decided she had to share these strange occurrences with Ben. That weekend, she told Ben about what the sitter had experienced. Faced with this reality, Ben could no longer put aside his disquiet and said Jamie that he had also had the same experience.

Suddenly they were interrupted by a noise. It sounded as though a ball bounced up and down. Ben went up to check on the children and found them all fast asleep. Bemused, the husband and wife had very different reactions. While Ben tried to dismiss the noise like the sound of an old house settling down, Jamie wasn't so confident. She started seriously wondering whether their house is haunted.

Determined to investigate, Jamie went to the local library to look up haunted homes in the area. Imagine her shock when the librarian helping her out told her that, not only had she (the librarian), grown up in a haunted house but that her haunted childhood home was the same one Jamie and her family were living in now. The librarian told Jamie that a little boy had fallen out of a second-floor window and died. The window belonged in the same room that Jamie's son Bridger now slept. Jamie got worried and asked the woman if she had ever felt afraid while living in that house. The woman answered in the negative. She said she believed that the ghost of the little boy just wanted some attention.

The activity in the house quieted down as the holidays came closer. One night, Jamie was sitting at her computer table, taking care of some paperwork. The computer switched off, and the monitor was dark. While working, she happened to glance up at the computer screen, and what she saw behind her froze her blood.

There was a dark, shrouded figure standing right behind her. She could see the shadowy figure reaching out. More frighteningly, she could feel the mysterious figure standing there. Scared out of her wits, Jamie called Ben at work. Almost incoherent with fear, she told Ben about what she had seen and felt. Ben tried to reassure her and promised her that he would be home as soon as possible. Jamie no longer believed that the ghost of a little boy was haunting the house, convinced that whatever lived in the house with them was evil.

After this, the strange phenomena stopped for some time, but Jamie's apprehensions didn't go away. She still felt the presence of evil in the house. Her suspicions were soon justified. Jamie had to pick up Tory after school one afternoon. The two were driving back home with Tory in the backseat and Jamie talking to her. Suddenly, out of nowhere, a barrel seemed to appear in the middle of the road. Jamie braked hard, but she'd been going too fast, and her vehicle flipped.

Jamie managed to crawl out of the vehicle. She was horrified to see Tory faced down on the ground pinned under the car. Her injuries were substantial, and she was rushed to the hospital immediately. When the couple arrived at the hospital, they received more bad news. The doctors thought that Tory's back broke. She had compression fractures in quite a few of her vertebrae. The Shea's were anguished and paralyzed with despair, wondering if their daughter would ever walk again.

Eventually, the hospital released Tory back to her parents. She was able to come home two weeks after the accident, just in time for Christmas. However, she was bedridden. It would take long months of recovery and physiotherapy before she could regain the use of her legs.

For several weeks afterward, Ben and Jamie were too focused on Tory's recovery to pay much attention to any unexplained activity. However, all that changed one night. Bridger came downstairs, complaining that the people in his room weren't letting him sleep. Disturbed, Jamie left her son with his father and went upstairs to check on the baby. Fortunately, the baby was sleeping like...well, a baby. He hadn't been disturbed by the noises that had frightened his brother. Unsettled, Jamie went back downstairs. She and Ben agreed that Bridger would sleep in their room that night.

All went well until the couple, and their son fell asleep. Suddenly, Jamie felt as though someone was tugging at her hair. Assuming her husband was teasing her, she asked him to stop. However, when she turned around to look, Ben was too far away to have done anything. While the couple looked at each other in shock, the bed started to shake violently. They jumped out of bed, and Jamie grabbed Bridger, while Ben went upstairs to get the baby. They spent the night in the living room with Tory, who had been sleeping there since her accident.

After enduring that night of terror, Ben and Jamie decided that they needed help to figure out what was going on in their house. They got in touch with the Central Arkansas Society for Paranormal Research or CASPR. The researchers agreed to come and check out the house. Once Tory was recovered enough to be moved, they sent her to the sitter's home along with her siblings.

That night, the investigators arrived. It was a husband and wife team, who also brought along their daughter. Alan Gold concentrated on finding evidence to verify the haunting. His wife Angela and their daughter Violet were psychics. Another paranormal investigator, Karen Shillings, accompanied them.

Karen had discovered that the house was more than two hundred years old, used as a way station, or a stopping point in long journeys, at one point in time. The fact that so many people had lived in or passed through the house made it a fertile ground for paranormal activity.

Angela and Violet decided to walk through the house to

figure out if they could feel anything. In the meantime, Alan set up his equipment, consisting mainly of cameras, in all the rooms. When the two women got to the second floor, they immediately had a bad feeling, and that feeling seemed to originate from Bridger's room. When the two psychics went into the room, Violet sensed that there was someone in the room beside them. At first, the presence seemed benign, perhaps frightened. She felt that it wanted to make contact with them but was too afraid.

Suddenly, the room filled with people, all talking loudly and giving a general feeling that the two women shouldn't be there. And then, all the loud noises with people talking disappeared as quickly as they had appeared. And the two women were fearful as the presence that came next in the room radiated pure evil and was devoid of any humanity. The women went back downstairs and told Jamie and Ben Shea about what they had found.

Angela decided to try to communicate with the different spirits. She pulled out an Ouija board. Ben wasn't too impressed and decided to handle the planchette off the board so that there would be no pushing or pulling. Angela started asking questions of the dark entity. At first, nothing happened. However, soon the planchette began to move. In response to the question, "What is your name?" the word "SETH" was spelled out. After a few more questions that got an indifferent response, Alan decided to ask the spirit when it had lived. The reply was chilling. "Never," it answered.

This answer shocked the investigators and the couple alike. They weren't dealing with ordinary spirits here. If Seth had never lived nor died, chances were that he was a demonic entity. Ben removed his fingers from the planchette and held on to his wife's hand. When he did that, the planchette started moving all by itself.

Alan asked the entity whether they had seen it. The answer was yes. Suddenly the planchette moved across the board and pointed towards the monitor that was connected to the camera upstairs. Alan switched on the monitor. Then the whole party watched in terror as a black shrouded figure moved from the hall into Bridger's room. It seemed to be floating at one time and swaying at another. Its movements were genuinely inhuman. Most of all, there was such a palpable sense of evil and malice emanating from the thing that everyone assembled in the living room downstairs could feel.

The investigators asked the Sheas if they had done anything, such as fortune-telling or conjuring, attracting the entity. The couple replied no. Then they remembered what they had found in Bridger's room before moving in – all the signs of an occult ceremony. The investigators looked concerned. They said that whoever had performed the rituals, left some sort of a gateway open, through which an entity such as Seth could get through, this is what they feared had happened.

Angela and Violet decided to perform a ritual cleansing to drive the evil spirit away. As though it had overheard their plans, the mood suddenly started making the planchette move again. Then the lights started flickering.

The two psychics lit sage and started chanting a prayer, asking God to protect the house and to help get rid of any negative spirits there. They let the smoke infuse every part of each room, starting in Bridger's room. They felt as though Seth was pushing against their chests, trying to get them to leave the house alone. They persevered, however, and after a protracted battle, were able to drive Seth away from the property. To ensure that he couldn't return, they drew a line of salt around the house. Since salt is considered a pure substance, it's believed that evil and negativity cannot cross it.

Once done, they went back in. The atmosphere in the house had changed completely. There was a lightness in the air, and the heavy feeling of oppression was gone. There was no sense of evil and menace that lived in the house alongside the family for so long. The evil entity was gone, but the human spirits who had been trapped there by it would stay. But there was no sense of evil from them, said the investigators.

The Sheas thanked the investigators profusely. A considerable problem resolved, and their children would now be safe. The kids got back the next day, and for the next several months, the family enjoyed living in the house with no evil presence or strange occurrences to mar their happiness. Tory had recovered entirely from the horrific accident and was back to normal. The family considered her recovery a miracle, considering how bad her injury had been. But sadly, these worry-free and happy days were not to last.

One weekend, after the kids had gone to bed, Jamie sat in the living room working. She was talking to Ben when suddenly they heard an unearthly sound behind them. They turned to see Bridger standing there. Stunned at the noise he had emitted, Jamie asked him if he was feeling all right. Bridger made no reply; he just stood at the bottom of the stairs and stared at his parents. Concerned, they quickly moved to him, and Jamie caught hold of his arms. All at once, it was as though Bridger had woken up. He stared at himself and looked at his parents in terror. "How did I get down here?" he asked them.

Ben and Jamie were horrified. They believed that the entity called Seth was gone. There had been no paranormal activity, no unexplained noises, and no sense of oppression in the house. Now it felt as though all of it came rushing back. Jamie left Bridger with Ben and ran upstairs to get Tory and Jackson. She ran into Jackson's room and grabbed him from the crib. As she ran out of the room, she heard voices. There were two of them, and they kept getting louder and louder. Terrified, she came out into the hallway facing away from Bridger's room and found Tory standing in front of her, transfixed with terror. When she ran towards her daughter, she realized that Tory was staring at something behind her.

Slowly, Jamie turned. The sight that met her eyes was unbelievable and genuinely horrifying. There, in the doorway of

Bridger's room, stood what looked like the same entity that they had driven out many months earlier. Jamie couldn't believe her eyes. It seemed as though Seth, and all the evil this maleficent presence had at its disposal, was back in their house.

Jamie grabbed Tory and ran down the stairs. She was terrified and kept thinking that they weren't going to go through this again. The family left the house right then and there and piled into their minivan. They knew that if they continued to live there, they would have to go through the terror all over again.

The very next day, the couple put their house on the market, and they moved to an apartment in the area. Soon after, Ben got his degree. And so the family made their home far away from what had once been their "dream home."

How the evil entity came back in the house, or how another entity got in, is something of a mystery. They speculated that the gateway that was opened by the people who had performed the occult rites before the Shea's moving in was too powerful and could not be properly closed. This evil void would be open permanently. Therefore, even though Seth was gone, other demonic entities could continue to find their way into the house. The family gave up on their dream house, realizing that the unfortunate place was going to stay haunted. And so they decided to make a new and happy life for their family elsewhere.

While a lot of skeptics may point out alternative explanations, there is no doubt whatsoever that something strange and unnatural was happening in that house. Credulity is not something that seems to be the case here, because Ben, at least, was not a believer. However, what he, his wife, and his children personally witnessed and underwent, changed his mind.

There can be a lot of reasons evil is present somewhere. Maybe it has been invited there, or perhaps it merely has existed in that place all along. One cannot speculate because there are limitless explanations. However, faith and good intent go a long way in removing this evil from our presence. Angela and Violet demonstrated this faith and useful purpose. They also showed strength and determination in the face of evil and were able to chase it out with the force of their conviction and good intentions. That is perhaps, the real lesson to be learned from this tale.

THINGS YOU WILL BUT SHOULD NOT GOOGLE

Humanity is a fascinating collection of creatures, but, as we all know, humans have inescapable darkness within them. The Internet has connected people like never before. It has become a reflection tool of all good as well as that which is terrifying. As you probably know, the Internet can thus be quite a dark, sinister place, and if you look in certain parts of it, you may find that a gut-wrenching reel of evil and horror is just a few clicks away.

Pain Olympics

Common sense often stops us from seeking out terrifying things online, but many of us just can't help giving in to our morbid curiosity. Be that as it may, there are a few specific things to be named that you should never look up, although you probably will.

To start things off, a lot of people have heard of something called the "Pain Olympics." Although the phenomenon may have died down somewhat in recent years, there was a time when "Did you watch the Pain Olympics?" was a question to frequently pop up at parties and other gatherings, asked by that one edgy individual who's always out to shock everybody.

In essence, although it got its name elsewhere, Pain Olympics is a video that went viral quite a few years ago online and has since become something of a mythical beast of the Internet. The original video shows two men engaging in a competition of who can cause the most shocking damage to his genitals. Although the footage is surprising, the original version was a clever piece of staged footage that was hosted by the online magazine BME, which focuses on extreme body modification.

However, the popularity of the video may have led to

numerous spin-offs and copycat videos created by different people over the years. The name "Pain Olympics" has thus become associated with all sorts of content, some of which may be even more shocking but real. Once you start browsing away, there's no telling where exactly you will land.

Creepy Confessions

While content such as that relies on direct shock value through gore, other stuff out there is just eerie and unsettling in its weirdness. While it's not something you should *not* search per se, the YouTube channel called "nasajim108" certainly has the qualities mentioned above. The description of the channel is straightforward and to the point. Stating, "These are a series of videos that my client requested to be released after his death."

The videos are short, and most of them titled as confessions of a dying NASA scientist. Usually revealing some truth about things such as the Illuminati secret society, theirs, and the US government's contact with extraterrestrial beings, subterranean alien species on Mars, and the like. The videos started uploading around nine years ago, and there are presently a total of fifteen uploads. While you'd expect all these videos to show recordings or interviews of the supposed NASA scientist, some of them do anything but, Some of the videos defy explanation.

Dark web

When it comes to strange, somewhat unsettling content, you will mostly be perfectly safe on YouTube. After all, this is a heavily moderated and tightly controlled platform. However, other places are just as easy to access, yet they are a whole different ballpark.

If you have been active on the Internet for at least a couple of years, the chances are good that you have heard of the dreaded 4chan forums. This website is entirely legal, and, at first glance, nothing seems to be wrong with the site, and it is perfectly normal for the most part. 4chan consists of numerous "boards," similar to Reddit's subreddits, which all focus on different topics to attract and gather around people with different interests, whether it's video games, politics, movies, pornography, or anything else people search for online.

However, 4chan's "Random" board, or "/b/," is where that which many people fear lies. This section of the website has but one simple rule: no illegal activity and content, such as child pornography. Virtually anything else goes; hardcore pornography, horrifying gore footage and other material, crime scene photos, truly off-the-rails sexual fetishes, animal abuse, torture, and virtually any other degradation that you can think of.

You may be surprised as it's possible that you didn't even know the simple truth that such material is by no means illegal to post or view, and it is up to individual websites to decide whether they will allow it or not. Seeing as

4chan/b/ is a surface link that is available to everyone online, any child with a computer can access it, and they probably do.

Believe it or not, the shocking content that you can find on this board should be the least of your worries. The true dark beauty of this place is the total anonymity it gives to its visitors, who simply refer to each other as "anons," which is short for anonymous.

As you can imagine, no rules and total anonymity do wonders towards bringing out the very worst in people. Visitors who frequent these boards do so only to unleash their darkest inner demons and frustrations against the world. Often involves ruining the lives of unsuspecting people, which is something of a pastime for bored veterans of the board. Some of these folks are very adept at programming and hacking, which makes them very dangerous in our day and age.

Most people who are at least somewhat acquainted with Internet culture already know that 4chan users are involved in quite a few high-profile hacking and dox attacks over the years. Allegedly, 4chan's /b/ board brought about the existence of the infamous hacker group "Anonymous" in the first place.

Any inexperienced Internet user who isn't all that savvy with computers and protecting personal information can be quite vulnerable if they wander into these parts of the web. All it takes is one slip, and someone could trick you and ruin much more than just your day.

In a twisted way, there seems to be a rudimentary code of "ethics" among the active visitors concerning these personal attacks. Stating they will not act upon private requests by other visitors. Meaning people will come to 4chan and post personal information about their enemies or just someone they don't like, hoping that someone on the board takes the data and uses it to hurt the target.

Perhaps even most terrifying for the average Joe would be the fact that 4chan has also been a place that murderers and other offenders have frequented. Such individuals sometimes come to the forum to brag about their foul deeds or even announce them before committing a crime.

One such case occurred in 2014 when a man by the name of David Kalac, arrested in the state of Washington, after turning himself in for the murder of his girlfriend. The thirty-three-year-old man had strangled the woman, taken photos of it, and posted them on 4chan. As if that wasn't enough insanity, he even talked about it in the thread he started on the board, posting that "it was way harder to strangle someone to death than it appears in the movies" and that "she fought so damn hard."

He then acknowledged in the same thread that he was going to leave her lying there with full knowledge that her thirteen-year-old son would come to find her dead after he comes home from school, which is what happened.

Although the murderer surrendered to the police, he stated on the website that it was his wish to be killed by law enforcement, committing a "suicide by cop." The police later confirmed that there was a high likelihood that Kalac was indeed the man who posted the thread.

People also suspected the 2015's Oregon mass shooter, who gunned down ten people at the Umpqua Community College, announced his rampage the day before on one of 4chan's boards. An ominous message in one of the threads simply stated, "Don't go to school tomorrow if you are in the Northwest." If one were to post such a message on YouTube, Facebook, or any similar site, you would expect scores of people decrying the poster as a madman, trying to stop it and imploring him not to go down that path, but not on 4chan. The anonymous message in question met with replies that cheered him on, urging him to do it.

As you can see, this is a place to avoid not just in the hope of not being exposed to terrible images and videos, but also for personal safety. 4chan and similar sites offer a devilish play-ground where the darkest aspects of man can shine and roam all but unchecked.

AFTERWORD

I hope you enjoyed these tales of true crime and paranormal horror stories. Now, you might be questioning whether the idea of demons, ghosts, and evil spirits are that farfetched. Many of the stories here occurred hundreds of years ago, but quite a few also took place as recently as the last decade. People had claimed to see supernatural beings for hundreds of years, dating back to the Egyptians when they buried their dead with some of their earthly possessions to take with them to the next life. However, some entities are stuck in this world. Unable to move past, lie beyond the void of life, and death.

Many mystics and psychics, while doing their energy readings, claim that when horrible trauma happens to people right before their death, not dying peacefully, their spirit is unable to cross over, left behind in limbo. When the soul has nowhere to go, and cannot join their loved ones and family members in the next world, the spirit becomes angry. Realizing the spirit does not have to obey the laws of the world that it is stuck in, and possessing incredible anger for what has happened along with the inability to move on, many spirits can turn violent. The violent spirits are the beings that were wronged and act out in aggressive, dangerous ways.

This book may just be a short compilation of real horror stories; however, these are not the only real horror stories that exist! This book is a compilation of true-crimes and unexplained phenomena from around the world. But it goes without saying, strange things happen every day and many are never reported to the police and media, or even to friends and family. That flickering light might be a little scarier now, and scratches coming from the ceiling might make you wonder if you should even move.